A Pocket Guide to Online Teaching

This pithy yet thorough book provides an evidence-based guide on how to prepare for online teaching, especially for those who are making a swift transition from face-to-face to online instruction.

Guided by the Model Teaching Criteria, this book covers important topics like how to adapt to expected and unexpected changes in teaching, how to evaluate yourself and your peers, and tips on working smarter/optimizing working practices with the resources available. The features of the book include:

- Practical examples exploring how to solve the typical problems of designing and instructing online courses.
- Interactive "Worked Examples" and "Working Smarter" callouts throughout the book, which offer practical demonstrations to help teachers learn new skills.
- Further reading and resources to build on knowledge about online education.
- End of chapter checklists that summarize suggestions about how to be a model online teacher.

This essential resource will provide support for teachers of all levels and disciplines, from novices to the most experienced, during the transition to online teaching.

Aaron S. Richmond is Professor of Educational Psychology at Metropolitan State University of Denver, USA. He studies how humans learn and develop and the application of this knowledge to classroom instruction and assessment.

Regan A. R. Gurung is Professor of Psychological Science and Director of the General Psychology Program at Oregon State University, USA. His research focuses on reducing prejudice, racism, and sexism, and the factors influencing learning.

Guy A. Boysen is Professor of Psychology at McKendree University, USA. His scholarship emphasizes the teaching of psychology, professional development of teachers, and stigma toward mental illness.

A Pocket Guide to Online Teaching
Translating the Evidence-Based Model Teaching Criteria

Aaron S. Richmond
Regan A. R. Gurung
Guy A. Boysen

NEW YORK AND LONDON

First published 2021
by Routledge
52 Vanderbilt Avenue, New York, NY 10017

and by Routledge
2 Park Square, Milton Park, Abingdon, Oxon, OX14 4RN

Routledge is an imprint of the Taylor & Francis Group, an informa business

© 2021 Aaron S. Richmond, Regan A. R. Gurung and Guy A. Boysen

The right of Aaron S. Richmond, Regan A. R. Gurung and Guy A. Boysen
to be identified as authors of this work has been asserted by them in
accordance with sections 77 and 78 of the Copyright, Designs and Patents
Act 1988.

All rights reserved. No part of this book may be reprinted or reproduced or
utilised in any form or by any electronic, mechanical, or other means, now
known or hereafter invented, including photocopying and recording, or in
any information storage or retrieval system, without permission in writing
from the publishers.

Trademark notice: Product or corporate names may be trademarks or
registered trademarks, and are used only for identification and explanation
without intent to infringe.

Library of Congress Cataloging-in-Publication Data
Names: Richmond, Aaron S., author. | Gurung, Regan A. R., author. | Boysen,
  Guy A., author.
Title: A pocket guide to online teaching : translating the evidence-based
  model teaching criteria / Aaron S. Richmond, Regan A. R. Gurung and
  Guy A. Boysen.
Description: First Edition. | New York : Routledge, 2021. | Includes
  bibliographical references and index.
Identifiers: LCCN 2020046933 (print) | LCCN 2020046934 (ebook) |
  ISBN 9780367646684 (Hardback) | ISBN 9780367649159 (Paperback) |
  ISBN 9781003126928 (eBook)
Subjects: LCSH: Web-based instruction—Handbooks, manuals, etc. |
  Teachers—Training of.
Classification: LCC LB1044.87 .R54 2021 (print) | LCC LB1044.87 (ebook) |
  DDC 378.1/7344678—dc23
LC record available at https://lccn.loc.gov/2020046933
LC ebook record available at https://lccn.loc.gov/2020046934

ISBN: 978-0-367-64668-4 (hbk)
ISBN: 978-0-367-64915-9 (pbk)
ISBN: 978-1-003-12692-8 (ebk)

Typeset in Times New Roman
by Apex CoVantage, LLC

We salute all the educators out there, both in K–12 and in higher education, who quickly, tirelessly, and passionately moved to remote learning and engaged in online education during the pandemic—2020 threw us all some major curveballs.

We sincerely thank you all and are glad to stand shoulder-to-shoulder with you. Your passion and persistent efforts inspire us.

Aaron, Regan, and Guy

Contents

List of Figures	x
List of Boxes	xi
Preface	xii

1 Apples and Oranges, But Still Fruit: Model Teaching Universals and Differences   1

Confessions of Three Skeptical Teachers 1
    The Background of Model Teaching 2
    What is Model Teaching? 3
    How is Teaching Different Online? 6
    Becoming a Model Online Teacher 7
*Stop, Think, Reflect: The Model Online Teaching Checklist
    for Training 8*
*Tips for Continued Learning About Model Online
    Teaching 9*

2 Student Interaction With Content   10

*Adapting Student Interaction With Content in an Online
    Course 10*
    Interaction With Content Through Student Learning
        Objectives 10
    The Syllabus and Your LMS is a Vehicle for Course
        Content 13
    Interaction With Content Depends on Course Design,
        Structure, and Clarity 14
    Model Online Teachers Use Course Templates to
        Organize Content 17

viii *Contents*

Special Considerations for Online Interactions With
Content 19
Broadening Instructional Methods 20
*Stop, Think, Reflect: The Model Online Teaching Checklist
for Student Interaction With Content 21*
*Tips for Continued Learning About Student Interaction With
Content 22*

3 Student-to-Student Interaction
23

*Adapting Student-to-Student Interaction: How to Build a
Community of Online Learners 23*
Establishing Student-to-Student Interaction Through
Discussions Forums 23
Fostering Student Community With Online
Discussion 24
Communicating Discussion Expectations 25
Fostering Student Learning With Online Discussion 26
Create Collaborative and Cooperative Online Learning
Opportunities 31
Establishing a Community of Learners Necessitates
Mitigation of Student-to-Student Conflict 33
*Stop, Think, Reflect: The Model Online Teaching Checklist
for Student-to-Student Interaction 35*
*Tips for Continued Learning About Student-to-Student
Interaction 35*

4 Instructor-to-Student Interaction
36

*Adapting to Online Instruction to Promote Instructor-to-
Student Interaction 36*
Use the Syllabus to Interact With Students 36
Use Various Instructional Methods and Skills to Interact
With Students 39
Practice Effective Online Teaching Skills 41
The Great Debate: Do Model Online Teachers use
Synchronous or Asynchronous Learning? 44
Interact With Students Via Student Evaluations of
Teaching 45
Interact With Students Through Student Feedback 46
*Stop, Think, Reflect: The Model Online Teaching Checklist
for Instructor-to-Student Interaction 47*
*Tips for Continued Learning About Online Instructor-to-
Student Interaction 48*

Contents ix

5 Online Assessment 49

How to Adapt Assessment to Online Instruction 49
   The Process of Assessing Student Learning Online 50
      Communicating Learning Objectives 50
      Alignment of Learning Objectives, Assignments, and
         Activities 51
      Providing Constructive Feedback Online 53
      Making Assessment-Based Changes 56
   Teaching Effectiveness Assessment Process 56
Stop, Think, Reflect: The Model Online Teaching Checklist
   for Online Assessment 59
Tips for Continued Learning About Online Assessment 60

References 61
Index 66

Figures

1.1	A List of Model Teaching Criteria and Subcriteria	4
2.1	CCOMFE Model for Online Course Design	15
2.2	Worked Example of How to Set Up Your Homepage	17
2.3	Worked Example of Consistent Style and Structure of Module Format	18

Boxes

2.1	Worked Example: Disciplinary Based SLOs for Psychology	12
3.1	Working Smarter: How to Facilitate Online Discussions	25
3.2	Worked Example: Writing Instructions for Discussion	28
3.3	Working Smarter: Online Discussion Rubric	29
3.4	Working Smarter: Strategies for Effective Asynchronous Collaborative Projects	32
3.5	Worked Example: Language for an Inclusive Online Class	34
4.1	Working Smarter: Learner- vs. Teacher-Centered Communication in the Syllabus	37
4.2	Worked Example: How to Incorporate Different Online Instructional Methods	40
4.3	Working Smarter: Online Rapport—Tricks of the Trade!	44
4.4	Working Smarter: When and Where to Use Synchronous vs. Asynchronous Learning	45
4.5	Working Smarter: Let Them See and Hear You	47
5.1	Worked Example: The ABCs of Writing Learning Objectives	52
5.2	Working Smarter: Using LMS Automatization	55
5.3	Worked Example: Writing Student Evaluation Items	58

Preface

Although there are many similarities between teaching online and teaching face-to-face, online instruction requires some specific pedagogical skills and consideration of unique challenges and dynamics. In the online world, technology forces instructors to use different skills or old skills in new ways. Also, content needs to be delivered on a different timeline and in a different format. Perhaps most importantly, students in online courses have different goals and expectations. Does the novice online teacher have to learn about these online intricacies piecemeal, or is there a broader philosophy to guide them into the online world? We spent many years thinking, writing, and researching what makes college instructors become model teachers. We dove into the research, did our own research, and formulated the Model Teaching Criteria for instructors of face-to-face classes. In this book we translate those criteria to the unique demands of online classes. Our goal in writing this book was to prepare *model online teachers*.

We wrote this book for teachers who are preparing to teach online, especially those who are transitioning from face-to-face teaching to online teaching for the first time. This includes graduate students, professionals who are new to teaching, and experienced face-to-face teachers. Model teaching practices are relevant across disciplines—they are about how you teach the content, not the content itself. As such, this book is intended for teachers from all academic domains.

Because the need to transition to online instruction sometime happens with shocking speed (one of your authors had four days to convert four in-person courses to an online format at the start of the COVID-19 pandemic), each chapter has features to enhance readability and utility. The features include short call-outs within the text that focus on various online model teaching skills and concepts. To find the key ideas, look for black boxes that contain model online teaching hacks (#MoT). We also feature examples of our own transitions to online teaching to help you anticipate the unanticipated, and every chapter contains "Working Smarter" and "Worked Example" boxes that expand on essential information from the text. Finally, all chapters end with a checklist that allows you to self-assess consistency with model online teaching practices

Preface xiii

and a short list of handpicked resources to help further your development as an online teacher.

We are grateful to Lucy McClune at Routledge for seeing the need for a book such as this and approaching us to take on the challenge of describing what it means to be model online teachers. We each have many individuals to thank. Aaron is thankful for all of his colleagues who share his love for teaching online and for his students who provide insightful feedback to improve the online learning experience. Regan is particularly thankful for the insights and good online counsel of Katherine McAlvage and Shannon Riggs, both part of Oregon State University's Ecampus program. Guy would like to thank his colleague Dr. Tami Eggleston at McKendree University for breaking the path that allowed him to wade into online instruction.

Writing a book on a short deadline during a pandemic was greatly advanced by having supportive partners. Aaron is eternally indebted to his wife, Amanda, and his three girls, Stella, Phoebe, and Violet; Regan is grateful for his wife, Martha, and his kids, Liam and Melina; and Guy is grateful for his wife, Marissa.

We hope this book helps you reach new heights of online teaching excellence.

1 Apples and Oranges, But Still Fruit

Model Teaching Universals and Differences

Confessions of Three Skeptical Teachers

At some point, each of the authors of this book had the same thought: "There is no way I am going to teach online." Regan remembers the first time he was asked to teach online. As a passionate teacher who enjoyed teaching large introductory classes of 300 students, as well as advanced classes of 25, he could not imagine teaching online. Why? He had preconceptions about what it would be like and could not imagine teaching without seeing his students live, face to face, numerous times a week. Guy too believed that technology would interfere with, rather than augment, what made him an effective teacher, and Aaron struggled with the thought that the rapport he had with his students would be somehow be lost online. That was then—now, we are converts.

Today, all three of us are firm believers in the merit of online teaching. While you would hope the authors of a book on online teaching support the practice, writing this book is not what changed our minds. First, we have examined the research. The evidence for the efficacy of online teaching is astounding and the benefits of a well-designed course are impossible to ignore. Second, from our years of personal experience, we have seen firsthand how a well-designed online course can lead to significant learning and, in many cases, provide some students with a better experience than they would have had in person. Of course, you will notice the caveat in each of those statements—"well-designed."

In this book we will provide you with the key ways to create and implement a well-designed online class. For many years we have immersed ourselves in defining, researching, and promoting the practices that define excellent teachers. In our own training to teach online we have taken advantage of the multiple resources about online teaching. There is a wealth of books, blogs, teaching center webpages, and even certified workshops on how to effectively teach online. Organizing all of this information so that it can benefit other teachers is challenging, but we have a way.

We bring you something different. Using the Model Teaching Criteria framework (Richmond et al., 2016), which is a set of six core principles characterizing model college and university teachers, we have synthesized the diverse guides and evidence-informed practices regarding online teaching. In this book, we offer a concise outline of the practices that will make you a model online

2 Apples and Oranges, But Still Fruit

teacher. Before discussing model online teaching, we introduce the general Model Teaching Criteria and the training needed to be a model teacher.

The Background of Model Teaching

If you are reading this book and starting at this chapter instead of jumping right ahead to the instructional tips, you want to be a good teacher—maybe even a great teacher. Definitions of great teaching exist, but college teachers rarely receive sufficient guidance for reaching such pinnacles (see Gurung et al., 2018, for a full review). Unlike K–12 education, college teachers typically do not receive pedagogical training, and this can make it a challenge to know where to begin as a teacher, let alone how to be great. We have had many conversations with graduate students who progressed from teaching assistants to instructors of record without training. Then, when those graduate students become faculty members, an advanced degree served as the only required evidence that they were ready to teach college courses full time for the next several decades. The assumption seems to be that if teachers possess knowledge, they should intuitively know how to pour it directly into the minds of students.

Of course, pouring content from your head into the minds of students is not the definition of good teaching. But what is? Behavior is complex, and it always influenced by multiple factors. Likewise, good teaching is comprised of multiple components. A few years ago, the three of us dove into the rich literature on teaching and pulled as many of these components together as we could. We built on the strong work of others: For two years, we worked with a committee of the Society for the Teaching of Psychology to establish the basic features of good college teaching. The committee studied what it meant to be a model teacher and concluded that there are six general criteria for model teaching (Richmond et al., 2014). This work led to checklist of model teaching practices that the three of us then revised and expanded into the Model Teaching Criteria (MTC, Richmond et al., 2016).

Before we unpack the criteria and illustrate how they can be useful in your progress toward online greatness, we need to discuss the sources of our teaching suggestions. You may be familiar with the terms "best practices" and "evidence-based," but they are slightly misleading. Classes vary in modality, size, composition, discipline, level, and college setting. There can be no "best" practice that works equally well in every context. We prefer the term "better." Similarly, "evidence-based" is not always possible. As three experienced pedagogical researchers, we can tell you that most prescriptions for good teaching in higher education are not (and cannot be) directly tested. There are too many variables to control, and classrooms experiments pose practical and ethical challenges. Learning is complex and research on education is imperfect, so we cannot claim that every suggestion in this book is evidence-based, and we feel it is false advertising to do so. We prefer the term "evidence-informed." In this book, we try to provide you with suggestions for better online teaching based on evidence-informed practices.

The sources of evidence for better teaching practices come from the many different groups working on understanding how learning works. Depending on discipline and training, your exposure to these areas will vary. When the three of us want to get up to date on teaching research, we first go to the major pedagogical journals in our home discipline of psychology: *Teaching of Psychology*, *Scholarship of Teaching and Learning in Psychology*, and *Psychology of Learning and Teaching*. All three journals publish research on the scholarship of teaching and learning (SoTL), which is commonly described as "the theoretical underpinnings of how we learn, the intentional, systematic, modifications of pedagogy, and assessments of resulting changes in learning" (Gurung & Landrum, 2015, p. 1). When SoTL is limited to and explicitly designed for specific disciplines, it is sometimes referred to as Disciplinary Based Educational Research (DBER). Nearly every academic discipline does SoTL, and this literature is the source of many evidence-informed teaching practices (Chickering & Gamson, 1987; Persellin & Daniels, 2014).

In addition to SoTL, researchers in the disciplines of education, educational psychology, and cognitive psychology also study learning, and scholars from a variety of disciplines consider their work part of the broader field of learning science (Benassi et al., 2014; Bransford et al., 1999). As if these varied sources of pedagogical knowledge were not enough, a separate body of research exclusively focuses on online teaching and learning, which is a topic largely skirted in the previously mentioned areas. Instructional designers, mainstays of academic technology departments and online campuses, have contributed a wealth of knowledge to inform online teaching practices (Dick et al., 2015; Smith & Ragan, 2005; Spector et al., 2015).

In our review of existing guides for online teaching, we note that most pull nicely from SoTL, DBER, learning sciences, and instructional design (e.g., Darby & Lang, 2019; Linder & Hayes, 2018; McCabe & Gonzales-Flores, 2017; Nilson & Goodson, 2018; Riggs, 2019; Stein & Wanstreet, 2017). Many of these guides resemble classic books about teaching, such as *Tools for Teaching* (Davis, 2009) and *Teaching Tips* (McKeachie & Svinicki, 2012). What they all have in common is that they outline specific teaching techniques, not an overarching model of what constitutes good teaching. We take a different tack and provide an interconnected structure of characteristics that together make a model teacher. You will find lots of teaching tips and tools in this book, but we present them as just pieces in a larger framework of model teaching.

What is Model Teaching?

In our view, and informed by the evidence, model teaching involves training, instructional methods, course content, syllabus design, assessment, and student evaluations. You will see these six criteria interwoven throughout this book, but we offer a brief overview of them here (see Richmond et al., 2016 for all the glorious details). Figure 1.1 summarizes the key components of this model.

4 *Apples and Oranges, But Still Fruit*

Training
- Continuing education on content knowledge
- Continuing education in pedagogical knowledge

Instructional Methods and Skills
- Varied instructional strategies
- Teaching skills of rapport and ethical teaching

Syllabus
- Learner-centered
- Positive and supportive tone

Assessment and Evaluation
- Align course activities, lessons, and assigments with learning objectives
- Use both summative and formative assessments

Student Evaluations of Teaching
- Regularly solicit formative and summative feedback
- Make changes based on student feedback

Course Content
- Course goals reflect breadth of your discipline
- Foster liberal arts skills (e.g., communication, critical thinking, information literacy)

Figure 1.1 A List of Model Teaching Criteria and Subcriteria (Richmond et al., 2014, 2016)

Model teachers are well-trained experts. At the most basic level, model teachers are credible authorities in their discipline. Teachers are most effective when they teach subjects that they have mastered. Achieving mastery requires up-to-date, specialized knowledge in that subject area (Boysen et al., 2015). As such, after earning their advanced degrees, model teachers demonstrate expertise through continued education and scholarship. Just like face-to-face teachers, online teachers must also follow these training guidelines.

In addition to their discipline-specific expertise, model teachers possess pedagogical expertise. Some graduate students have been part of training programs such as Preparing Future Faculty or department training as part of being a teaching assistant. Faculty may occasionally attend professional development sessions about teaching and learning offered at their college, or they may read about teaching trends in the *Chronicle for Higher Education* or *Inside Higher Education*. These types of ad hoc training are not enough. Model teachers learn about teaching through self-directed professional development, but they also receive formal training. There is no substitute for attending a course on pedagogy. Whether it is an online workshop, a multiday conference, or a full

Apples and Oranges, But Still Fruit 5

academic course, such training is essential for model teachers to establish and maintain expertise on pedagogical theory and practice.

As a result of their training, model teachers follow fundamental practices in the design, instruction, and improvement of their courses—these are the other five components of model teaching. The purpose of this book is to outline these model teaching practices as their relate to the context of online instruction. As can be expected, most of the subcriteria that made up the original Model Teaching Criteria (Richmond et al., 2016) are directly or indirectly applicable to online teaching. In following chapters, we explicitly use the model teaching framework to help you learn about online teaching.

Model teachers use learner-centered principles to design their syllabi (see Chapters 2 and 3). Their syllabi communicate to students who they are as a teacher, define the relationship between the students and the teacher, provide a permanent record for future use, and serve as a cognitive map and learning tool for the course (Richmond et al., 2016). Model teachers' syllabi are transparent and complete. They have detailed policies on grading, academic misconduct, attendance, plagiarism, etc., to communicate expectations to students.

Model teachers intentionally select course content (see Chapter 2). Whenever relevant, they align content to disciplinary guidelines about essential learning goals. Model teachers also go beyond their disciplines. They help students develop liberal arts skills related to communication, critical thinking, and collaboration.

Model teachers use varied instructional methods (see Chapter 4). It is clear from even a quick look at various teaching tips books (e.g., Davis, 2009) that there are a variety of ways to teach. Online teaching can utilize a wealth of instructional methods that go beyond posting lecture slides, asking questions, and then giving a test. Some of the better, evidence-informed methods include collaborative learning, problem-based learning, and just-in-time-teaching, all of which require active student engagement. Developed primarily in the context of face-to-face learning, each of these techniques can also be adapted to online learning. When implementing these methods, model teachers exhibit skills such as student-teacher rapport, active listening, and technological competence.

Model teachers are engaged in the process of assessing student learning (see Chapter 5). They write learning objectives to guide instruction, assess student achievement of those objectives, reflect on the outcomes, and revise instruction based on that reflection. Model teachers know how to take advantage of both evaluation directness (i.e., aligning assessments and evaluations with specific learning objectives within a course) and evaluation utility (i.e., providing timely constructive feedback, Boysen et al., 2015).

Model teachers use student evaluations of teaching for improvement (see Chapters 4 and 5). They collect formal and informal feedback from students and use that information to make changes to their instruction and the course. There is debate about the use of student evaluations to make administrative decisions about teachers, but model teachers recognize the important and unique perspective students have on the functioning of courses (Boysen et al., 2015).

6 *Apples and Oranges, But Still Fruit*

How is Teaching Different Online?

Good teaching is good teaching, regardless of modality, right? There are strong arguments for the universality of good teaching across modalities (Chickering & Ehrmann, 1996; Nilson & Goodson, 2018). But, like all things, effective online teaching is both contextually and situationally dependent. What may work for teaching an introductory level class may not work for teaching an upper-level class. Students in Athens, Georgia, will not approach class in the same way as students in Athens, Ohio, let alone Athens, Greece—and students from each location may be in the same online class. There are some unique elements to online teaching (and online students) that call for the modifications of fundamental aspects of in-person teaching. The good news is that there are few, if any, brand new skills to learn for online teaching (aside from some of the technological skills). If you have the fundamentals of being a good in-person teacher, then you can be a good online teacher. To this end, we aim to help you grow into a model online teacher (MoT).

> **#MoTs recognize that teaching is both contextually and situationally dependent.**

Despite their shared characteristics, online teaching is different from face-to-face teaching in obvious and not so obvious ways. Most online classes do not meet at scheduled times or on scheduled days. This asynchrony calls for a different approach to course design. Instead of big blocks of time in a classroom with students, online classes stretch out across the week. Students are accessing and interacting with course material and communicating with you 24 hours a day, seven days a week. Because online teaching and learning are unbound from the calendar and the clock, you have to be more intentional in how you carve up your course content and how you carve up your time for contact with students.

Not seeing students face to face leads to one of the biggest shocks for in-person instructors transitioning to online instruction. In-person instructors rely on the face-to-face contact to share information and check student understanding. If an assignment is not clear in the syllabus, you know someone will ask a question about it or you can go into more detail in person. You also, if you are like most faculty, make changes to your lessons close to class time and perhaps even during class. In stark contrast to this in-person, in-the-moment flexibility, when teaching online, you launch a complete class all at once. When your online course opens, every week and every assignment should be designed and ready for implementation.

Online teaching requires a completely different workflow (Riggs, 2019). In order to have a fully designed course by day one of the term, you have to spend a lot of time a priori. You might assume that you can launch a few weeks of material while you work on the rest, but most colleges do not allow instructors to launch courses that are only partially designed. "What about academic freedom?" you cry. Well, here is another big difference with online teaching. Most colleges and universities require online faculty to go through training on how to design an online course. Together with training, many colleges will also assign an instructional designer to work on the course. There is often a standard course template that must be used. Your freedom is restricted, but see this for the blessing it is. Unlike the general lack of guidance for in-person teaching, most colleges make sure you are very well supported before you teach an online class.

> **#MoTs have different workflow and time flexibility.**

In today's world of higher education, students taking online courses are becoming similar to those who enroll in in-person classes, but there are still some key differences among many online students. On average, online students are older, more likely to be working full time, and more likely to be parents. Online learning provides the flexibility that mature working parents need. Most online courses are student-driven, rather than instructor-driven, enterprises. This means that online courses often require students to spend more time on task (Brewer & Brewer, 2015), which is why students often learn more from well-designed online classes than comparable in-person classes.

Whereas the synchrony, workflow (for both student and teacher), and student characteristics differ between in-person and online courses, other key areas remain the same. Online and in-person classes can and should have the same learning goals and academic rigor. Just like in-person classes, learning in online classes is tied to the quality of instruction (Tallent-Runnels et al., 2006). Quality of instruction is tied to training, and that is where this book can play a role.

Becoming a Model Online Teacher

We developed the Model Teacher Criteria from the perspective of face-to-face instruction. Although we believe that the six criteria apply to all types of instruction, we recognize that online teaching has some unique challenges and differences. Correspondingly, we looked at all of the criteria and selected those that explicitly relate to online teaching. We then looked for a concise way to present the six criteria and multiple subcriteria. Reflecting on what it takes to be a model online teacher in particular, we have divided them up into the three areas of interactions that typically define online instruction. Specifically, we have organized the Model Teaching Criteria into chapters on student interactions with course content (see Chapter 2), student interactions with other students (see Chapter 3), and student interactions with the instructor (see Chapter 4). In addition, we outline the assessment processes needed to evaluate the performance of students and the teacher (see Chapter 5).

8   *Apples and Oranges, But Still Fruit*

We start with all the model criteria that apply to student-to-content interaction. This natural starting point acknowledges that the online learner sees their task as interacting with the content via a very different format than traditional in-person learners. Instead of relying on live lectures and print textbooks, students can interact with content in every modality deliverable by technology. In many ways, students interact with content via the instructor. Thus, a major portion of the book focuses on instructor-to-student interactions, discussing the many ways online instructors communicate with students. Online learning is not just a student interacting with posted material and watching lectures. Students also interact with each other. Online teachers pay particular attention to student interactions as they work to achieve the course learning outcomes. To determine if all this interaction has had the intended effect, teachers assess student learning and ask for student feedback on their teaching, and those evaluation processes are how we conclude this book.

> **#MoTs use effective instructional methods and skills, are experts in pedagogy and course content, design effective syllabi, engage in assessment, and use student feedback.**

Stop, Think, Reflect: The Model Online Teaching Checklist for Training

As it is the essence of continued professional development, we conclude this chapter with a self-evaluation checklist that will allow you to determine your current consistency with model online teaching practices. First, we want you to self-assess. Second, identify areas of training or activities that you could improve upon. Third, choose one or two things to try out. Fourth, repeat. As the three of us will attest, this process of instructional improvement never stops.

- ☐ Your official transcripts reflect course work related to online pedagogical training.
- ☐ You have given presentations at regional or national conferences related to online pedagogical strategies.
- ☐ You have peer-reviewed publications related to online pedagogical strategies (e.g., SoTL articles).
- ☐ You participate in continuing education related to content areas taught online.
- ☐ You participate in continuing education related to online pedagogical strategies.
- ☐ You publicly disseminate information about online teaching innovations and outcomes (e.g., publications and presentations).

Tips for Continued Learning About Model Online Teaching

As our book is meant to be an introduction to online teaching, each chapter will include some more advanced sources to continue your professional development.

- If you want to conduct your own research on teaching, check out McKinney's (2018) *Enhancing Learning Through the Scholarship of Teaching and Learning*.
- To learn more about MTC, read Richmond and colleagues (2016), *An Evidence-based Guide to College and University Teaching: Developing the Model Teacher*.

2 Student Interaction With Content

The COVID-19 pandemic caused students and faculty immeasurable stress as face-to-face courses rapidly moved online. Students who signed up to go to a class in person now had to contend with learning from home, often in their childhood bedrooms, no less. Behavior patterns had to change. Students who would normally read the textbook, go to class, find their regular spots, settle into their seats, and then spend 50 to 110 minutes taking notes (perhaps with a few distractions thrown in) now had to learn in new ways. Faculty who could rely on preparing lessons just before class had to put more thought into their preparation and the new ways that students would being interacting with course content.

For those of us who teach large introductory courses, this instructional shift may have been an unexpected blessing. In contrast to sitting in a 400-seat auditorium, students would now be sitting face-to-face with faculty on a screen. This switch, while approximating online teaching, was not the same as a fully developed online course and nicely illustrated how student interactions with content are different based on course modality. Students who intentionally sign up for online classes, unlike students who were surprised by the remote instruction of 2020, expect to have different interactions with their teacher and course content. In this chapter we focus on how students interact with content via student learning objectives, the syllabus, course design, and the course website.

Adapting Student Interaction With Content in an Online Course

Interaction With Content Through Student Learning Objectives

Every course offered in higher education has a catalog description. In most cases, you will not be the person who wrote that description, but reading it is the place to start when selecting content for an online course. Even if you have a syllabus and materials from a face-to-face version of the course, reading the catalog description is still a good time to consider the key question: What knowledge and skills do you want your students to gain from your course?

Student Interaction With Content 11

Do not make the mistake of picking a textbook first. We did that as novice teachers—rookie mistake. The core of a course is not a textbook, it is the student learning objectives (SLOs). SLOs are what you need to develop first because they answer the question of what students need to know (see Chapter 5 on how to create SLOs). SLOs impact every aspect of a course, so it is important to make them visible to students. In online classes especially, it is critical to have your SLOs prominently and widely displayed. They should be easy to find in your syllabus (more on that in a bit), but they also need to be featured across the learning management system (LMS). For many students, the first exposure to course SLOs will be when they log into your LMS. Before you launch your course to the world, learning activities for every week should be specified, and each learning activity should be tied back to the SLOs for your course.

When planning course content, fine tuning your SLOs is time well spent. Many academic disciplines have SLOs for undergraduate programs and some even have SLOs for individual courses. For example, the American Historical Association participated in a global initiative to create consistent SLOs spanning different countries and disciplines, called the Tuning Project. For history, the core competencies and learning outcomes can be viewed at www.historians.org/teaching-and-learning/current-projects/tuning. In psychology, the American Psychological Association (APA) has *Guidelines for the Undergraduate Psychology Major 2.0* (APA, 2013). As illustrated in Box 2.1, it is important to not only create well-crafted SLOs but also to create assessments that require students to interact with content to achieve said SLOs.

Academic departments also have SLOs for majors and minors. Your course SLOs should relate to the department outcomes because each department ideally maps out which courses in the curriculum address which department outcome. If you have inherited a course, you will have the course SLOs to work with. If you are designing a brand-new course, spend some time on deciding which SLOs are most relevant for your course. For a crash course in SLOs, see the indispensable *Assessing Student Learning* (Suskie, 2018).

Most SLOs for a course address major theories or concepts that students should know. For example, in Introductory Psychology, one SLO is for students to "Identify basic concepts and research findings." This often leads instructors to cover a set number of chapters in a textbook. In semester-long introductory courses, instructors cover anywhere from 12 to 14 chapters. Yes, some even try to cover all 16 chapters in a traditional textbook. The important element here is that content is more than just settling on a number of chapters of information. Instead, you need to be able to get your students to truly interact with that content.

When writing SLOs, an easy way to ensure good interactions with the content is to consider Bloom's Revised Taxonomy by Anderson and colleagues (2001). The taxonomy describes the different levels at which students interact with content (seen in italics here). Some teachers believe learning is just

12 Student Interaction With Content

Box 2.1 Worked Example: Disciplinary Based SLOs for Psychology

The APA sets the learning goal for undergraduate psychology majors to develop their knowledge base of the field, and this goal leads to specific SLOs like those listed in the following. To illustrate the concept of backwards design, we have worked out how these three outcomes could lead to specific assessments and then the possible methods for interacting with content to achieve the outcomes.

SLO 1: Describe key concepts, principles, and overarching themes in psychology.

- *Assessment:* Multiple-choice tests or quizzes, asynchronous discussion forum
- *Interaction With Content:* Open-education resource textbook, online scavenger hunt

SLO 2: Develop a working knowledge of psychology's content domains.

- *Assessment:* Reflection paper, team debate between behaviorism and cognitive psychology
- *Interaction With Content:* Textbook, synchronous and asynchronous lessons, visit Virtual Psychology Museum

SLO 3: Describe applications of psychology.

- *Assessment:* Synchronous discussion, applied analysis paper, quizzes
- *Interaction With Content:* TEDx Talk, YouTube videos, asynchronous lessons, recorded interviews of past psychology graduates

---

Remembering with the ability to recognize and recall facts, or *Understanding* demonstrated by summarizing, explaining, or inferring. However, the taxonomy adds the additional steps of *Applying* (e.g., implementing), *Analyzing* (organizing and differentiating), *Evaluating* (e.g., critiquing), and *Creating* (e.g., generating and producing). When you write your SLOs, keep these distinctions in mind.

The moment you aim to have your SLOs span the range of Bloom's Taxonomy, you will note that you move away from covering content and, instead, urge students to think about content a more meaningful level. To ensure this deeper processing of content you need to provide adequate assignments (see Chapter 4 on how to accomplish this goal). Especially as you get your students to analyze or create, you move beyond what is commonly used in introductory classes—the multiple-choice exam—to a greater use of discussion and essay writing. Fortunately, the online class is the perfect venue to utilize these forms of interaction with content.

For some courses, instructors must pay close attention to the role played by the course in the broader curriculum. If you are teaching Chemistry 101, for example, your role may be to prepare students for Chemistry 201. Instructors also have to look beyond discipline-specific content. For example, your course may need to satisfy general education learning outcomes for your college or other graduation requirements. Some colleges have requirements that match their specific mission (e.g., sustainability) and these may need to feature in your course. There are also learning outcomes that are part of a liberal arts education. For example, the Association of American Colleges and Universities have defined a set of essential learning outcomes that are content agnostic (AACU, n.d.). They include critical thinking, communication, quantitative literacy, and civic engagement.

While you design your content and fine tune your SLOs, aim to be an inclusive teacher. The events of early 2020—the deaths of George Floyd and Breonna Taylor in particular—brought issues of inequality to the fore, which directly relates to how students interact with content. Designing your course to be accessible to a diverse range of students is paramount. When you select content, make sure you include diverse voices. Too many courses only include the writings of White men or feature the colonizing voice. To teach inclusively is to show students diverse voices (Gannon, 2020). In addition to the content you select, ensure you do not make assumptions about your students, especially in terms of what their diverse backgrounds have prepared them for. In online classes, where you may not see your students, it is also easy to make assumptions about their behavior. Consider adding inclusive dialogues and icebreakers (see Chapter 3). To learn more about inclusivity, consult with the office of multicultural affairs and diversity experts on your campus.

The Syllabus and Your LMS is a Vehicle for Course Content

Once you have your SLOs fine-tuned, you are ready to move on to the next stage of backwards design. How will your students interact with the content to get to the outcomes you have outlined? Your syllabus is a focal point of an online class as it provides you with your map to designing the look and feel of your course within the LMS (we circle back to the syllabus in Chapter 4 for more). Your syllabus and your course LMS should clearly show learning outcomes and the associated learning activities and assignments (see Box 2.1 for an example). In short, students need to know WHAT they are doing and WHY they are doing it, and the best vehicle to convey this information is the syllabus. See Chapters 3 and 4 for how to best design an effective online syllabus.

14   *Student Interaction With Content*

Whether in the syllabus or in the modules within the LMS, it is important to take a learner-centered approach in order to increase students' interaction with course content. One way to do this is to create autonomy and choice within your course via the syllabus (Richmond, 2016). One way to do this is by assigning an activity that requires students to provide some course content. For example, rather than the instructor being the source of information, students can provide examples or applications of course concepts from the news or from their own lives. You may also have students come up with course policies and procedures on how to interact with one another. Finally, using collaborative projects (see Chapter 3 for more details) will force students to interact with content and one another.

When you teach online, the course LMS serves as equal partner with the syllabus in laying out course content. You have undoubtedly told students many times, "It's in the syllabus!" Well, in an online class you can modify that to "It's in the LMS!" Even though your syllabus is your cognitive map for course content, you now have a number of different LMS tools to inform students about what they have to do and to guide them through the learning process. Although a good syllabus should have some key content, the course LMS can provide even greater detail for students in a more interactive medium. A good syllabus starts with the class SLOs and clearly states what the students have to do to earn a grade (what are the different assignments, how much do each count for). It also describes the course activities (discussions, group work) and provides a detailed schedule. In online courses, this essential syllabus content is unpacked throughout the LMS. In a face-to-face class, the students have to sift through the syllabus to find out what to do. For online students, simply logging in to the course LMS should reveal the entire course and guide students through the learning process.

> **#MoTs use the syllabus as a cognitive map of course content.**

Interaction With Content Depends on Course Design, Structure, and Clarity

Students deserve a well-designed learning experience. *Design* is the key word here and a particularly important concept when teaching online. Consider one end of a continuum. A student wants to learn about biology. They buy a used, relatively recent, introductory biology textbook. They read the book, answer the questions at the end of the chapter, and even work with material on Quizlet, Idorecall, Brainscape, or similar software. They will have interacted with the same content that many students taking a class for credit would have, but the experience will lack the key elements of a well-designed class.

To be a model online teacher your course needs to *have a* design. This recommendation may sound strange. Don't all courses have a design? The research on face-to-face classes shows this is not always the case. For example, Homa et al. (2013) examined over 100 syllabi from across the U.S. and found that approximately 20% of them did not include student learning outcomes. The syllabi also showed little alignment of content, instruction, and assessment. The first step in effective online teaching is designing your course well. There is an entire field of study related to instructional design, and online course instructors often have instructional designers help put a course together. Even if you do not have access to an instructional designer, model online teachers need to know the basics of course design (Nilson & Goodson, 2018). This involves taking a close look at what you want your students to learn and having a clear plan of how they will learn it by interacting with your course.

#MoTs design each module or unit to follow similar structure and patterns to provide a cognitive map for students.

There is an overarching principle here that transcends many of the how-to guides and nicely exemplifies many aspects of being a model online teacher. When you examine the experiences of faculty members and students, those who have better experiences are in classes characterized by six factors: compassion, clarity, organization, multiple facets, flexibility, and engagement—in short, they are CCOMFE (see Figure 2.1). These six factors provide a prescription for online teaching and learning, nicely echoing evidence-based practices for

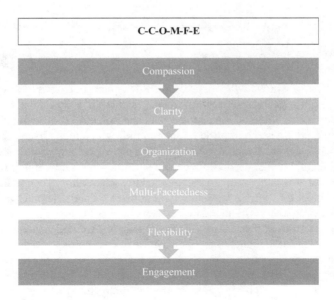

Figure 2.1 CCOMFE Model for Online Course Design

16   *Student Interaction With Content*

good face-to-face and online teaching in general (Richmond et al., 2016; Riggs, 2019). We allude to and directly address many of these six components in this chapter and those that follow (see Chapter 4 on how to increase compassion, flexibility, and engagement). The key is to be CCOMFE when designing your course in general, and especially when planning how your students will interact with course content.

When one considers training to teach face-to-face, few programs and guides (if any) spend time on organization of the LMS because the main course document is the syllabus. In online teaching, there is a host of better-practices for LMS set up, and here is where instructional designers come in. Instructional design scholarship and organizations such as Quality Matters provide a long and useful list of guidelines for how a LMS should be set up. But, if you do not have access to these resources, here are a few ideas that will allow you to organize your SLOs to ensure students interact with content.

Students can better interact with content when the rationale and the instructions are clear (i.e., clarity in CCOMFE). Unlike a face-to-face class where you can answer questions immediately as students raise their hands, most online classes are asynchronous. You may not be available, or even awake, when a student has a question. Your challenge is to anticipate students' questions and avoid even prompting them by making your course structure *clear* and *consistent*. The best way to do this include explicit instructions and design every module to follow a similar pattern and structure. Unclear expectations cause stress, and instructors can support students by providing them with complete, well-structured content.

> **#MoTs are compassionate, clear, organized, multifaceted, flexible, and engaging.**

Regardless of which LMS you use, a well-designed course has a Home Page, optimally with a "Start Here" section where you overview the course. Your Start Here section should include the course nuts and bolts: A link to your syllabus, netiquette guidelines (i.e., online etiquette guiding postings, discussions, and student behavior), the structure of the course, your expectations, and essentially anything the student should know before starting. Share how many modules you have and how many weeks are contained in each module. The modules will include content for students to read, watch, or listen to; activities such as discussions or ways students will interact with each other (see Chapter 3); methods for interacting with their instructor (see Chapter 4); and graded assignments (see Chapter 5). The Home Page of an Introduction to Psychology course at Oregon State University is seen in Figure 2.2. It is designed to be inviting, attractive, and eye-catching, with all the key information right there. Students know where they start. There is a vivid picture of the instructor to welcome the student,

Student Interaction With Content 17

Figure 2.2 Worked Example of How to Set Up Your Homepage

personable text, and a simple, uncluttered layout. Along the left edge you also see the key course components.

To provide a transparent course, you should also use a consistent pattern in how you display information. Every module should look the same and all should map on to the assignments described in the syllabus. Figure 2.3 shows you a sample module list. Note how it is described in terms of Weeks. This way you do not have to keep changing the dates every semester. It also has clear categories of items. For each module there is an overview of a lesson, content videos, quizzes, and active reading questions.

Model Online Teachers Use Course Templates to Organize Content

The great news for online instructors is that most campuses have entire departments devoted to supporting online teaching. Even if you are not affiliated with a Southern New Hampshire University or Oregon State University, two of the top online programs in the nation, you can still take advantage of the tools they have devised to aid online instructors. As discussed in Chapter 1 on training, your university may provide you with Quality Matters training or even have self-paced training modules to help you develop your course. When it comes to

18 *Student Interaction With Content*

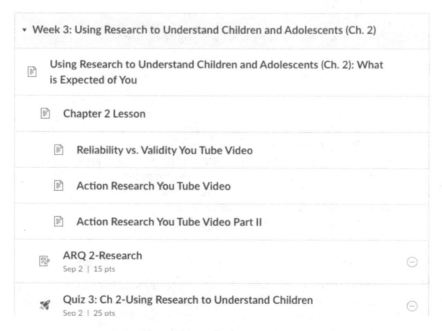

Figure 2.3 Worked Example of Consistent Style and Structure of Module Format

incorporating the key elements discussed in this chapter that relate to the LMS and syllabus, the single best resource is the course shell.

Course shells are skeleton online classes that are developed with all the best practices already built in. All you do is add content. If you are lucky, or just looking in the right places (such as reading this far in the book), you can also find user-friendly guides to setting up your class. For example, a self-paced course from Oregon State University is available for anyone developing and teaching a remote course during COVID (https://canvas.oregonstate.edu/courses/1794174). This course is non-facilitated, and you can work through the contents at your own pace, based on your own needs and interests. If you are using Canvas as your LMS, you can use the templates available here: https://learn.oregonstate.edu/canvas/canvas-faculty-tools/canvas-templates.

Special Considerations for Online Interactions With Content

In the context of interacting with content, you need to consider students' direct interactions, such as reading a text or article, as well as indirect interactions. Indirect interactions include how students are thinking about the material. Whether you post a video for them to watch or have them read a chapter in a book, do not stop there. You need to design ways for students to interact with that material.

Riggs (2019) provides a wide range of specific ways to have online students interact with content. For example, when your students read an article, have them write a summary of it or create a slideshow with the key takeaways. You could have them record a short video or audio clip of them summarizing the article. Audio and video assignments provide the online student with novel and exciting ways to interact with the material. You can also have them create a concept map or mind map (see the free online app Mind Map), create an infographic (e.g., CANVA), write a critique or op-ed piece, or even write quiz or exam questions on the material. Many specific ways to foster student-student interaction (see Chapter 3) also serve the purpose of helping students interact more with the material.

The teaching community provides a wealth of examples for how to design interactions with content. Seek out similar-minded teachers with blogs, websites, and social media accounts (are you following the three of us yet on Twitter? @AaronSRichmond, @GuyBoysen, @ReganARGurung). For example, you can follow the example of a TEDx Talk Regan recorded. His 17-minute talk is great to have students in Introductory Psychology courses get a bird's eye view of the field. It is also a nice way to show that not all scientists are old White men. In the talk he picked essential elements of psychology and stitched it together to share some key principles. Not only is it a useful example and model for what your students can do as an assignment (how would they summarize the key points of your course in ten minutes?), but it also forces additional interaction with the material. The clip comes with a self-guided, ten-item multiple-choice quiz and additional questions for discussion. The entire self-contained lesson can be found here: https://ed.ted.com/on/JafZNxLS#review.

20 *Student Interaction With Content*

As illustrated by Regan's video example, getting students to reflect on the material is key. Many classic face-to-face classroom assessment techniques (Angelo & Cross, 1993) also come in handy online. Require students to post what they are most or least confident about, what they found unclear, or what they found most helpful. There are also numerous guides to student reflection that can be modified for class use (e.g., Ryan, 2012). You may provide a simple prompt asking the student to first summarize what they read and then to evaluate the material. You may want students to apply what they have read to areas of their lives or other courses. You may want students to explicitly critique their readings. Some other suggestions include having students provide evidence and make inferences, think about changes in their feelings and thoughts over time, make connections between current and prior learning, and imagine future applications of the content. Whichever route you decide to go, the bottom line is to provide a scaffolding for exploration and an explicit charge to engage in the material. Your guiding questions show students how to do it, and optimally you provide a rubric and examples of prototypical good answers. In short, model online teachers have clear assignments telling students what to do with content.

> **#MoTs have students engage in reflection papers to allow them to interact with course content.**

Broadening Instructional Methods

If you have taught many face-to-face courses and perhaps attended many faculty development workshops, the checklist for your syllabi and ways to use a LMS may not seem too groundbreaking. Having taught before builds confidence, but online teaching is not the same. Whereas your personality, delivery, voice, energy, and excitement can enliven a class when you are in front of them two or three times a week, your LMS and written words have to do the bulk of the enlivening online. Yes, recorded audio and video messages can go a long way, but online instruction requires a broadening of instructional methods. You should not be recording hour-long lecture videos (multiple short 6-minute videos are best). And you should not just have students read a chapter and take a quiz on it. You need to think broader.

In order to achieve the E in CCOMFE, you have to be creative in finding ways to get your students to interact and engage with the content, and that often involves using new teaching methods. You want to design your course for a range of learners. Whereas you can read faces, body language, and field questions live in a face-to-face class, you cannot do that easily online. Your instructional methods should fit different abilities, a concept referred to as Universal Design for Learning or UDL (Tobin & Behling, 2018). Once discussed primarily in relation to students with disabilities, proponents of UDL now portray it as a way to increase accessibility for all students by providing opportunities to interact with content in multiple ways and then demonstrate learning in multiple ways.

UDL principles immediately provide ideas for how to have students interact with content in different ways. The basic idea is to provide multiple ways for your students to engage with the material you have. This idea is based on research from neuroscience that shows that there are different neural systems involved in learning. Some networks are specifically tied to recognition of material and relating to past memories of knowledge. Others are related to feelings or affect. By having diverse ways for students to interact with content (e.g., text, video, podcast), you are helping activate students' neural networks. These strategies may include providing ways for students to customize the display of information. Take the example of captioning videos. Whereas this will help a student who has trouble hearing, it will also help the student with caregiving responsibilities who must silently watch a course video while caring for a sleeping child.

Stop, Think, Reflect: The Model Online Teaching Checklist for Student Interaction With Content

For many students, learning involves getting new content. In model online teaching, this content is provided in many different ways. In online teaching, even more so than face-to-face teaching, the syllabus and LMS layout for the course lays the major framework for structuring students' learning and for how they are to interact with content. In this chapter we laid out the main considerations in planning how your students will interact with content. A student's interaction with content must involve more than just listening to recorded lectures or even sitting in on synchronous live lectures. Interacting with content is more than just reading a book, whether online or in print. Working with content also takes place in every interaction with the instructor and with other students, two main areas we turn to next. To assess your own readiness on topics covered in this chapter, reflect on the extent to which you would agree or disagree with each of the statements that follow.

☐ Your course learning goals reflect the breadth of content in your discipline.
☐ You foster the development of student written communication skills.
☐ You foster the development of student critical thinking skills.
☐ You foster the development of student information literacy skills.
☐ You foster the development of student oral communication skills.
☐ You infuse ethical issues throughout your teaching.
☐ You infuse diversity issues throughout your teaching.
☐ Your syllabus reflects an intentional link of SLOs to class activities, assignments, and assessments.
☐ Your syllabus is strategically organized to accomplish course goals.
☐ Your syllabus provides clear and complete information about course goals and requirements.
☐ Your syllabus provides clear and complete information about course grading/assessment.

Tips for Continued Learning About Student Interaction With Content

- Shannon Riggs' (2019) *Thrive Online: A New Approach to Building Confidence and Expertise as an Online Educator*, is a thoughtful, easy to read guide to the major considerations that go into online teaching.
- If you have never encountered the term Universal Design for Learning, Tobin and Behling's (2018) *Reach Everyone, Teach Everyone: Universal Design for Learning in Higher Education* is a recent publication with a strong overview of different elements of UDL.

3 Student-to-Student Interaction

Walk by a college classroom before class starts. Peek in. You are likely to see students lost in silent, isolated contemplation of their digital devices. Ideally, when the teacher takes charge, this staid environment turns into a rich cacophony as students break out of isolation and work together to find solutions to interesting and challenging questions. Online learning should be the same. Unlike the stereotype of the online student working in isolation on their computer, a critical component of teaching online is fostering interaction among students. In fact, although online teaching is much quieter than in-person teaching as far as decibels go, it is much louder when you consider the volume of interactive student output. Although designing online courses with many ways for students to interact with the content is essential, a large part of your design energy should be also be spent on helping students interact with each other.

Adapting Student-to-Student Interaction: How to Build a Community of Online Learners

Definitions of good teaching often emphasize how much students like a teacher—think of student evaluations and student-led teaching awards. No one could deny the importance of instructors' rapport with students (see Chapter 4). However, good teaching also includes building rapport *between* your students. If your students see your class as an enjoyable and safe community, then they are more likely to be involved with the material and with each other. Community building is an important part of online teaching. There are several ways in which you can build community, but the two predominant methods are through the use of well-designed and implemented discussion forums and cooperative and collaborative learning activities.

Establishing Student-to-Student Interaction Through Discussions Forums

The COVID-19 pandemic of 2020 led to a massive switch from in-person to online learning. As debate emerged about how long the moratorium on in-person courses should last, some critics characterized online coursework as

24 *Student-to-Student Interaction*

glorified correspondence courses or assumed that online classes consist solely of watching lecture videos. Contrary to these stereotypes, in well-designed online courses, students constantly interact as part of the learning process. Discussion forums are the essential hub for these interactions. As such, model online teachers foster discussions and help students work effectively with their classmates during the discussions.

Teachers can design online courses that require different levels of student interaction. One useful metaphor is to think about student interaction in an online course as being like a playground, a baseball game, or a symphony (Parker, 2013). Courses with little student interaction are like a playground. In such courses, students engage with content independently with the help of the instructor, which is like children using different playground equipment under the watchful eye of a teacher. More interactive courses are like baseball, where the teacher is the coach and the students are players who encourage and guide each other but are still functioning in largely independent roles on the field. Finally, truly collaborative courses are like symphonies; the teacher serves as a conductor who ensures that everyone plays their part, and without effective collaboration, the final product is failure. Learning can occur in each of these designs, but model online teachers strive toward building courses where student collaboration supports and improves learning.

> **#MoTs promote online discussion and foster students' abilities to work effectively and collaborate with others.**

Fostering Student Community With Online Discussion

Discussion forums are where much of the learning and student-to-student interactions occur in online courses, and model online teachers build community among students to make that learning more enjoyable and effective. A standard first assignment in online courses is for students to introduce themselves. Effective icebreaker assignments make an impersonal class personal. An endless variety of icebreakers exist, but the best ones allow students to get to know each other, share important information about themselves, and, ideally, make connections between their lives and course content. For example, a generic icebreaker could ask student to post a picture of themselves or something that represents themselves, share why they are in college, and list one thing they are excited to learn about in the course. Icebreakers can seem hokey, which can lead to a certain amount of dread about doing them. However, model online teachers design and implement meaningful icebreakers that teach students a basic skill of working with others; namely, building rapport improves teamwork.

Another community-building method is to create an ongoing discussion forum just for socialization purposes. McCabe and Gonzales-Flores (2017, pp. 211–212) provide an example of the language that sets the right tone when prompting participation in a social forum—"Welcome to our virtual coffee shop. Pull up a stool, order a latte or a chai, and let us know what is on your mind. This is just for fun—so relax and enjoy." Just as students in face-to-face classes might bond in the halls before or after class, online students can bond by hanging out in socially focused discussion forums.

Even when the focus of discussions is not explicitly social, community building can occur. Stommel (2020) suggests instructors facilitating discussion should try to build a community of care, ask genuine open-ended questions, wait for answers, let conversations wander, and model what it looks like to be wrong. Finally, aim to make your listening visible by acknowledging comments in your posts and responses and urge students to as well. See Chapter 4 on different methods of delivering comments and feedback.

Communicating Discussion Expectations

Effective online collaboration requires teachers to establish expectations beyond "introduce yourself." Model online teachers also set clear expectations for the format and function of course discussions. Unnatural as it may seem, discussions need due dates. Just as a good facilitator would tell a group working in person, "You have ten minutes to reach consensus on this issue," a good online teacher informs students when their online discussion posts are due. There may even be multiple due dates during a given week, with the first being for initial posts to the discussion topic and the second date being for responses to other students' posts. Teachers should also set expectations for frequency and timing of discussion posts. Without such direction, there will be a tendency for online discussions to consist of single posts made right before the deadline. Such a trend kills discussion. What is the minimum number of posts students need to show engagement? How far in advance of the deadline should posts generally be? Teachers who have specific answers to these questions should make them known to students before discussions start. As described in Box 3.1, Stein and Wanstreet (2017) provide key strategies to facilitate your online discussions.

Box 3.1 Working Smarter: How to Facilitate Online Discussions

1. Prompt learners to justify their responses by tying it back to a class reading or an article they read and then cite as support.
2. Ask students to explicitly acknowledge the contributions of others as a way of building ownership and keeping plagiarism in check.
3. Push for originality and statements or expressions of ideas that go beyond regurgitating the text.
4. Have students connect their discussion to resources beyond the required course material.
5. Have students connect content to real-world experiences to apply their knowledge with relevant examples.

26 *Student-to-Student Interaction*

Effective online discussions are more than timely; they consist of a dialog rather than discrete points. Many classroom discussions consist of a series of unrelated student comments directed at the teacher, and the same dynamic can emerge during online discussions. Rather than being a dialog between students, discussion posts can become mini essays designed only as an object for the teacher to read and grade. Model teachers break up this dynamic. One method to increase dialog between students is to set explicit expectations for how many posts must be responses to other students. In addition, teachers can stipulate that responses to other students must be substantive. For example, a teacher might explain that agreement or disagreement is not enough, justifications are also needed. Or teachers can encourage students to ask their classmates questions.

Promoting online discussion and fostering collaboration requires teachers to be present on the discussion boards so they can monitor student work and provide direction (Darby & Lang, 2019; McCabe & Gonzales-Flores, 2017). Of course, being present online is related to student-instructor contact, but it is also necessary to shape discussion. There are many ways teachers can use their presence on the discussion boards to maximize student-to-student contact (Vai & Sosulski, 2011). For example, they can ask specific students to contribute if they are not participating. They can stimulate further discussion by asking questions. To stimulate student-to-student interactions, teachers can ask for comments about specific students' posts. In general, teachers should model openness to varied perspectives so that students feel comfortable sharing their ideas.

Fostering Student Learning With Online Discussion

Social media is now the location for public discussion about an array of topics, some important and some not. Anyone who has decided to take a five-minute break to scroll through their social media feed and emerged, dazed, from a 30-minute trance knows that online chatter can be engrossing. However, being engrossed in a discussion is not the same as learning from a discussion. We could easily spend 30 minutes reading comments on a single tweet about Bob Dylan's singing ability and come away knowing nothing new about Bob or singing. Discussion fails when it is active but empty.

Model online teachers encourage student discussion as a means of connecting students but also as a means of learning. Allowing students to connect is important, but discussion is ultimately a pedagogical technique. If learning does not occur, the technique has failed. As such, model online teachers use student-to-student contact on discussion boards as an active learning technique to engage students with course material.

#MoTs engage students in course material.

Returning to the analogy of online courses being like a symphony with the teacher as conductor, even the best musicians will not produce Beethoven's Ninth Symphony unless they have sheet music to learn and time to rehearse. Discussion boards are where students rehearse course content. Online discussions allow students to actively test their acquisition of knowledge and their achievement of the skills needed to be successful in the course. As conductor of this symphony of learning, instructors must provide stimulating ways for students to actively engage with course material during discussion.

Topics for online discussion boards are as diverse as course subjects, but good discussion prompts share certain characteristics. First, discussion prompts should facilitate the sharing of multiple perspectives. Discussion does not flow if students can simply post the right answer and be done. Second, good prompts force students to use higher-level cognitive skills such as application, analysis, synthesis, and evaluation. Little learning will occur if students can just copy and paste information into the discussion board rather than making their own intellectual contributions. Third, prompts should be meaningful. Give students discussion material they will care about. For example, topics might be connected to current events, to students' lives, or to students' future goals. Finally, discussion prompts should mimic work that is central to the discipline. As much as possible, have students do the work of professionals in the discipline. For example, in a marketing course, students might discuss ways to improve an advertising campaign. In an education course, students might discuss ways to solve various classroom discipline problems. In a research methods course, students might evaluate the validity of published studies.

In addition to specifying discussion format expectations such as due dates and post frequency, teachers should set expectations for the intellectual content of discussions. If the focus of discussion needs to be on application, analysis, synthesis, or some other intellectual task, explicitly build that into the instructions (see Box 3.2). Teachers might also consider setting expectations for originality in students' posts. If a student can pass merely by parroting the ideas of other students, they are not truly engaged in active learning. In addition, sometimes it is more valuable to stimulate others' thinking than to demonstrate personal knowledge. As such, teachers should encourage posts that lead to additional discussion such as asking questions or posing problems.

You have established discussion expectations. You have given students engaging discussion prompts. Students have discussed. What now? The answer to this question depends on the quality of the discussion. If students have met expectations, they should be rewarded and encouraged to continue their good work. If students have not met expectations, they need guidance on how to improve. Setting up and facilitating online discussions are just the first steps. Teachers must also provide students feedback on their discussion performance.

Box 3.2 Worked Example: Writing Instructions for Discussion

Discussion should promote learning by engaging students in the intellectual processes of a discipline. Effective discussion prompts clearly outline how students should engage in that process. In these examples, the discussion prompts relate to the same intellectual topic but ask students to engage with the material in different ways.

Ineffective Prompt That Only Specifies a Course Topic

• Discuss Pavlov's theory of classical conditioning and Skinner's theory of operant conditioning.

Application Prompt

• Imagine that you are placed in charge of 5-year-old boy with severe behavioral problems. The child rarely speaks, constantly rocks back and forth, and engages in self-harm behaviors, such as hitting himself in the head when he is not allowed to rock back and forth. How could you use Pavlov's theory of classical conditioning and Skinner's theory of operant conditioning to change this boy's behavior so that it is healthier and more functional?

Analysis Prompt

• Imagine that you are placed in charge of 5-year-old boy with severe behavioral problems, such as lack of speech, repetitive behaviors, and self-harm. Outline why Pavlov's theory of classical conditioning or Skinner's theory of operant conditioning would be more useful in changing the boy's behaviors.

Synthesis Prompt

• Imagine that you are placed in charge of 5-year-old boy with severe behavioral problems such as lack of speech, repetitive behaviors, and self-harm. You consider using Pavlov's theory of classical conditioning and Skinner's theory of operant conditioning to change the boy's behaviors. What would be the key similarities in the effective implementation of the two theories in this case? What would be the key differences?

#MoTs provide constructive feedback to students about their achievement of discussion expectations.

There are two main ways that teachers can give students feedback on discussion performance: Grades and rubric scores. Discussion is an important way for students to engage in active learning in online courses. As such, include it in the gradebook. Meaningful participation in online discussions should have a meaningful impact on students' final grades, as should failure to participate. Although there is not a universally accepted amount that discussions should count toward final grades, one rule of thumb is that students are unlikely to take discussion seriously if it cannot influence their final marks by at least one full letter grade.

Grades are useful for getting students' attention, but more detailed feedback is needed to guide improvement. This is where rubrics are invaluable. Consider the online discussion rubric in Box 3.3. The domains of performance that the teacher will evaluate are specified in the rows of the rubric. The columns specify the levels of performance that define how well the student has performed on each domain. Of course, teachers can add or subtract domains and levels of performance as fits their goals. In addition, when integrating rubrics into an LMS, there will be options for associating points with each cell in the rubric, and teachers can weight the domains to fit the importance of various discussion goals.

Rubrics are an essential tool for model teachers. A detailed rubric helps convey expectations to students. Teachers can make the rubrics visible to students in the LMS and attach them to assignments so that students can self-evaluate before they submit work. Teachers might even require a self- or peer-evaluation with the rubric to ensure that they are familiar with the expectations. In addition, rubrics allow teachers to provide students with feedback on how well they have performed in relation to those expectations. Simple letter grades do not tell students what to do differently. In contrast, a completed rubric tells students exactly where their work can be improved and how. Moreover, some LMSs include an option where each rubric score can be associated with automatic feedback that tells what student needs to do to improve (see Box 3.3 on how to create an online discussion rubric).

Box 3.3 Working Smarter: Online Discussion Rubric

Discussion task	Meets expectations	Needs improvement	Unacceptable
Frequency	Participates in every thread but does not dominate discussion	Participates in most threads or needs to let others participate more	Does not regularly participate or dominates discussions
Automatic feedback	*Participation is great. Keep up the good work!*	*Boost how much you participate a little in the future/hold back slightly and let others participate in the future.*	*You need to participate more/ You need to let others contribute.*

30   *Student-to-Student Interaction*

Discussion task	Meets expectations	Needs improvement	Unacceptable
Responsiveness to others	Regularly responds to the comments of others to offer questions, clarification, or additional information	Does not regularly respond to others	Does not respond to others or responses are off topic
Automatic feedback	*Great job responding to others!*	*Respond to what other students say a bit more.*	*Read and respond to other students.*
Timeliness	Always meets deadlines and posts early enough for others to respond	Mostly meets deadlines and posts early enough for others to respond	Posts past deadlines or too late for others to respond
Automatic feedback	*Way to stay on task!*	*Work on posting a little bit earlier to be part of the discussion.*	*Make sure to post by the deadline. Others need to see your posts in order to discuss them.*
Professionalism	Tone, language, and content of responses are respectful and classroom appropriate	Tone, language, or content of responses shows slight inappropriateness	Tone, language, or content of responses is not respectful or classroom appropriate
Automatic feedback	*Way to be professional!*	*Consider appropriateness before posting in the future.*	*You should only be posting appropriate, professional material during discussions.*
Content	Comments show understanding of content, correct applications, and attempts to further understanding	Comments show some understanding of content and mostly correct applications	Comments show little understanding of content or mostly incorrect applications
Automatic feedback	*Good work making your comments relevant!*	*Be sure to check the accuracy of your work before posting it.*	*Be sure to get a basic understanding of the material before trying to discuss it.*

Discussion boards are a microcosm of online courses in general. The goal is for students to learn. But to achieve that goal, teachers must set up a productive, communal workspace for students. Students need clear standards for what is expected of them, meaningful tasks to work on, and feedback on their progress. When designed the right way, learning will occur. Moreover, it will be enjoyable, because students will all be able to see their contributions to the symphony of learning occurring in the discussions and in the greater course.

Create Collaborative and Cooperative Online Learning Opportunities

Consistent with the mantra of online teaching, the course design choices you make go a long way toward effective collaboration and cooperation. As we mention in Chapter 4, good online instruction is not merely recording your lessons using some screen capturing app. To really focus on student-to-student interaction, model online teachers create collaborative projects. Collaborative learning is a well-established high-impact practice in higher education (see Chapter 4 for further discussion). Collaborating is more than having conversations about course content. True collaborative learning involves students both learning to work and solve problems with other students, and developing the practice of paying attention to the viewpoints and opinions of diverse others (Kuh, 2008). In other words, collaborations need to have a learning goal that directs purposeful student interactions.

There are several ways that model online teachers use collaborative learning to increase student-to-student interactions. For instance, they may hold creative brainstorming sessions to share course content (see Chapter 2). Or they may have students record a presentation and have other students provide feedback using software such as VoiceThread. Model online teachers also use team debates, team virtual scavenger hunts, and so on. Collaborative projects could include team-based problem solving, debates, wikis, social bookmarking, online field trips, shared case studies, homework forums, or jigsaw activities. Collaborative projects could involve as few as two students to 20 or more. Regardless of the type of collaborative learning activity you may use, to ensure success, keep groups small, create an equitable peer evaluation for group work (i.e., to prevent slacking), form diverse groups, and build strong group interdependence. Moreover, as illustrated in Box 3.4, Riggs (2019) suggests there are some key strategies for effective online implementation.

Moving beyond general strategies for online collaborative projects, it is also important to structure your projects with specific goals in mind. First, prepare your students for group work. To do this, make sure you align group work with your SLOs, provide a clear rationale for using group work, and carefully consider the size of the group and how you put students into groups (three to four students per group is optimal). It is also a good idea to give students a checklist so they can monitor their progress and their deliverables. Any material you can create to help facilitate group processes (e.g., teach group work skills, establish

Box 3.4 Working Smarter: Strategies for Effective Asynchronous Collaborative Projects

- Provide direct instruction on expectations for the collaboration.
- Require communication that is visible to all.
- Allow sufficient time for each activity.
- Put into place milestones (required or optional) that carve the project down into manageable chunks, each with a deliverable and a due date.
- Utilize low- or no-stakes assessments early in the course to give students exposure and practice with how you will assess the final collaborative work.
- Be explicit about how you will grade participation of the group (e.g., a rubric).
- Provide students with a way to reflect and comment on the group process.
- Establish a clear process for dealing with conflict.
- Ensure you have made the purpose clear and linked the purpose and activity to the course learning goals.
- Provide prompt, meaningful feedback, often mid-activity if needed.

norms, develop a group contract) will make the process more productive and enjoyable for all. Assigning roles in the group is one particularly helpful way to structure group process.

Model online teachers also use cooperative learning activities to promote student-to-student interactions. In cooperative online learning, students work individually and then share the collection of individual results with other students. Cooperative learning tends to be more short-term, where students work together in ad hoc groups within a class period to achieve a learning goal (Major, 2015). The main difference between it and collaborative learning is that cooperative learning is more structured, with each student having a specific role to play in the group that is necessary for task completion. For example, many model online teachers use cooperative learning for group- or team-based research projects, where each group member is assigned a specific role (e.g., literature review specialist, copy editor, data and analysis expert). Another example is implementing student quiz teams. Have students work in small groups, with each student responsible for a specific set of information; then quiz the students individually and the highest scoring team receives extra credit.

In the end, using collaborative and cooperative learning forces students to interact with one another. Whether it be synchronous or asynchronous, through these methods, students will begin to feel like they are a part of a learning community because throughout the process they get to know their fellow classmates.

Establishing a Community of Learners Necessitates Mitigation of Student-to-Student Conflict

Whether you are teaching an online course for the first time or the umpteenth time, you have to be ready when things do not go as you planned. The relative detachment and anonymity associated with online communication means that anger and offense is never more than one ill-conceived reply away. To maintain a professional learning environment, online teachers set expectations for the tone of discussion. At the most basic level, they explicitly forbid uncivil behavior (see Box 3.1). Discussion needs to maintain basic professionalism, but do the students have to sound like a bunch of professors? Opinions differ on professional writing standards for online discussions, but a good rule of thumb is that discussion boards function best if students can communicate in the same conversational tone that teachers expect during in-person discussions. Although teachers with learning goals related to writing or professional communication may increase their expectations, writing standards should not be so high that they discourage frequent, lively participation.

A key part of an enjoyable online environment is safety. Make sure that your class has clear-cut prescriptions for online etiquette (netiquette). This will ensure smoother and more enjoyable discussions. Box 3.5 is a worked example that describes language for creating a safe online zone. You may also want to add language on creating an inclusive class.

Another potential way to identify student-to-student conflict is by instituting frequent formative assessments. Early in the semester, have students complete a brief survey reflecting on the quality of their interactions with their classmates. If you have a discussion due early, immediately ask students to reflect on their learning and their satisfaction with it. Frequent, short evaluations can help you keep your fingers on the pulse of student–student interactions and the community in your classroom.

> **#MoTs change their course syllabi, materials, lesson plans, or teaching methods based on formal and informal assessment.**

There are other situations that create student-to-student conflict that you need to be prepared for. The most common occurrence of this is when world events take place that may put your assignments that are designed to have students interact with one another into a different context. In online teaching, you should have your class prepared by the time it is launched. This means that all your student-to-student interaction prompts will also be set. Watch out for changes

34 *Student-to-Student Interaction*

Box 3.5 Worked Example: Language for an Inclusive Online Class

Expectations for Student Conduct

Student conduct is governed by the university's policies, as explained in the Student Conduct Code (https://beav.es/codeofconduct). Students are expected to conduct themselves in the course (e.g., on discussion boards, email postings) in compliance with the university's regulations regarding civility. Students are not allowed to post inappropriate material, SPAM the class, use offensive language, or engage in online flaming.

Creating an Inclusive Classroom

Although 99% of our genes are similar, we have different backgrounds, values, attitudes, and histories. All students are welcome in this class regardless of race/ethnicity, gender identities, gender expressions, sexual orientation, socio-economic status, age, disabilities, religion, regional background, veteran status, citizenship status, nationality, and other diverse identities that we each bring to class. I acknowledge another source for difference: Not all people have had the same resources or opportunities as others, resulting in inequalities. My goal is to create a comfortable, fertile learning environment, with equitable treatment for all. We are partners in learning, and I will expend every effort to help you succeed. If circumstance has disadvantaged you, I am dedicated to rectifying this wrong. I will treat each of you with respect and dignity and I would welcome you return the effort with me and your classmates.

---

that may be needed in the middle of the semester that may affect these interactions. In 2020, it was not only COVID-19 that changed our worldviews, but also the killing of George Floyd and the resulting protests nationwide that influenced us all, and students of color in particular, that changed the tone of interactions. Being able to adapt and evolve by revising assignments that may be difficult to face in light of these issues is key.

In addition, an assignment you created may be interpreted the wrong way given the current state of affairs. Paying attention to how students interact with each other in response to prompts is paramount. Be prepared to step in and address issues you may see. If a student posts potentially offensive material, you need to have a plan of action ready (most likely addressing the student privately first). If a distasteful posting is missed or not addressed, the quality of student-to-student interactions can greatly suffer.

Stop, Think, Reflect: The Model Online Teaching Checklist for Student-to-Student Interaction

In a face-to-face class, facilitating student-to-student interactions seems easy. Students are sitting right there, side by side, so they just need to turn a little bit and start talking. In contrast, there is an element of anonymity that seems to work against you when you are trying to encourage student-to-student interaction online. You have to be more strategic. To help you intentionally plan those crucial student-to-student interactions, complete this checklist and consider where you could boost student contact. Better yet, ask your students these questions and see what they say. If you find gaps, try to change something in your online courses that allows you to achieve the unchecked items.

- ☐ Your students interact frequently.
- ☐ You promote online discussion.
- ☐ You foster students' ability to work effectively and collaborate with others.
- ☐ You engage students in course material.
- ☐ You use multiple instructional methods based on students' needs and course objectives.
- ☐ You provide constructive feedback to students about their achievement of online discussion expectations.
- ☐ You change course syllabi, materials, lesson plans, or teaching methods based on formal and informal assessment.

Tips for Continued Learning About Student-to-Student Interaction

- Check out this resource by Bart (2011), "Fostering Student Interaction in the Online Classroom," on how to foster student-to-student interactions.
- Read Palloff and Pratt's (2007) *Building Online Learning Communities: Effective Strategies for the Virtual Classroom* to collect some great ideas.
- Even though it is not just about student-to-student interaction, you might want to read Stavredes' (2011) book on *Effective Online Teaching*.

4 Instructor-to-Student Interaction

One of the most enjoyable parts of teaching is to walk into a classroom, make eye contact with your students, engage in conversation, read the body language of students, and laugh, smile, and enjoy one another's company. Ironically, we currently write this book while socially distancing and teaching remotely from home due to COVID-19. How do we capture the magic of face-to-face interactions with students online? Just like in face-to-face interaction, there are several evidence-informed instructional strategies that you may use to create and maintain educational magic. First, it starts with the syllabus—that is what your students initially see. Second, there are several different instructional methods and skills that will promote positive and impactful interactions with your students. Third, model teachers use both synchronous and asynchronous interactions with their students. Fourth, it may be a surprise, but one of the best ways to interact with students is through your feedback and how you communicate your findings of student evaluations of your teaching.

Adapting to Online Instruction to Promote Instructor-to-Student Interaction

Use the Syllabus to Interact With Students

Just like in face-to-face courses, the online course syllabus serves as a contract (Robinson Wolf et al., 2014), as a permanent record (Richmond et al., 2014), and as a cognitive map and learning tool (Parkes & Harris, 2002). Chapter 2 discusses the syllabus as an introduction to course content, but it is also an introduction to the instructor. One of the most important elements of the syllabus is that it serves as a mechanism to interact with your students by providing an official communicative device (Richmond et al., 2016). If you think about it, the syllabus is likely the first interactions between you and your students. What will this first impression look like? Will your students think, "Wow this is going to be a long semester. They clearly know nothing about technology and seem dull as hell," or will they say "Meh, it's a general ed class so I'm stuck in here," or "Wow, this teacher really cares and I can't wait to get started. They are tech savvy, organized, and hilarious." If you are aiming for "Wow, this teacher really cares!", Bain (2004) suggests that the syllabus is an excellent opportunity to garner the trust of your students by demonstrating that the syllabus is more than just a list of assignments and dates.

So, what elements of the syllabus can help you communicate who you are? Most researchers suggest that including your contact information, a teaching philosophy, and student and instructor behavioral learning objectives are good ideas, and that the tone of your syllabus communicates many different things to your students. Box 4.1 illustrates how you may interact with your students through the syllabus.

Box 4.1 Working Smarter: Learner- vs. Teacher-Centered Communication in the Syllabus

Contact Information

Teacher-Centered: You have limited contact availability and methods of contacting you.

Learner-Centered: You include office hours, email address, office phone (possibly include anonymous texting service), and any other means of communication (e.g., Twitter, video conferencing). You indicate whether you are available outside of office hours and include a scheduling app service so that students can sign up to meet you.

Teaching Philosophy

Teacher-Centered: No teaching philosophy is included.

Learner-Centered: You include a statement about your philosophy that includes the why, what, and how of your teaching.

Student and Teacher Behavioral Expectations

Teacher-Centered: You only communicate to your students what is expected of them. For example, "Turn in work on time."

Learner-Centered: You seize the opportunity to communicate what you expect of students and, more importantly, what they can expect of you.

Your Tone

Teacher-Centered: Your language is authoritarian, harsh, and shrill, with a focus on punitive action and consequences.

Learner-Centered: You incorporate a friendly, warm, positive, rewarding, and supportive tone throughout the syllabus. For instance, you write in first person and use personal pronouns. You use inclusive language rather than exclusive language and avoid condescending and confrontational language.

Note: These best practices are selected and adapted from Richmond (2016).

---

38 *Instructor-to-Student Interaction*

As illustrated in Box 4.1, each element of the syllabus communicates something specific about you as a teacher and how you will interact with your students. For instance, having multiple synchronous and asynchronous methods for students to communicate with you about the course expresses that you care about their well-being and success in the course, and that you want to interact with your students often. Or, including a course-specific description of your teaching philosophy in the syllabus communicates that you have thought deeply about the course and spent a lot of time developing the course, as opposed to just "mailing it in." Sulik and Keys (2014) suggest that "syllabi . . . do more than communicate course objectives and the means for achieving them. Syllabi (re)socialize students for success in the college setting by establishing student-teacher roles and norms and setting the tone for classroom interactions" (p. 151). Therefore, by providing clear and concise student AND teacher expectations, you are establishing a culture within your class and communicating to your students that not only do you have high expectations for them, but that they should equally have high expectations for you and that you will do your best to work as hard as they do. Last, by writing your syllabus in a supportive, kind, and friendly tone, your students will have better rapport with you (Richmond et al., 2016). For example, just by changing the words "Office Hours" to "Student Hours" could cause your students to be motivated and connected to you (Harnish & Bridges, 2011, p. 323).

> **#MoTs use an introductory video to interact with students about the syllabus, course structure, and culture of the class.**

How do instructors interact with students about the syllabus? One of the more effective ways to introduce yourself, class expectations, and class policies (i.e., what is in the syllabus) is an introductory video lesson that is typically delivered the first. In this lesson, you should explain all of the elements of the course (i.e., assignments, calendar, assessments) but also other elements such as how to succeed in the course, and where students can go for help (e.g., online tutoring). You should also have one document (a traditional syllabus) in PDF format available for students (i.e., the one you send out the week before school so that students can get a great first impression of you) and incorporate each of the key syllabus elements (e.g., grading policies, summary of important due dates, course alignment map, teaching philosophy) within pages in the LMS. The reason it is so important to have your syllabus in so many different formats is because of accessibility issues. If you have it in multiple formats, it is easier for students with either visual or auditory difficulties to access and understand the information (Rao et al., 2015). The reason to covey it in video format (i.e., use Loom, Camtasia, or any other video capturing apps) is that this will further codify the student's first impression of you and will begin the positive and productive interaction between the two of you.

In the end, why go through all this trouble of developing a model syllabus? Without out a doubt, syllabi are major vehicles of communication and their tone can play an important role in this process. Like it or not, the syllabus conveys who you are and what you represent, and they can cause students to make judgments about you and the course. With a model syllabus guiding them, students will likely engage more in the course and follow directions better (Kim & Ekachai, 2020). Therefore, if you want to be a model online teacher, then your syllabus should communicate that you are one.

Use Various Instructional Methods and Skills to Interact With Students

One of the most impactful ways teachers interact with their students is through their instructional methods. First, let us say it right here: Model online instructional strategies are not just posting recorded videos of your lectures! Rather, model online teachers learn to embrace varied pedagogical approaches that focus on engaging students in the learning process instead of focusing on what works best for the instructor (Boysen et al., 2015; Kim & Bonk, 2006). In Boysen and colleagues' (2015) study of model teaching criteria, 75% of teachers reported using varied instructional methods—the idea of the straight-lecture or straight-discussion teachers seems to be false. Kim and Bonk found that only 11% of online instructors relied solely on traditional lecture-based teacher-directed instruction; most instructors also use some form of active learning, such as cooperative or collaborative learning, problem-based learning, Socratic discussion, case-based instruction, role-playing, coaching/mentoring, guided learning, or exploratory learning. The point is, there is no one educational method that fits all students and all types of courses.

While it is beyond the scope of this book to have an exhaustive list of the different online instructional methods, we wanted to take some time to work with some examples on how you can implement some of the most evidence-based methods, as demonstrated by award-winning online instructors (Martin et al., 2019). As illustrated in Box 4.2, there are several different ways to implement online instructional strategies. The question then becomes, when and where do I use these various instructional methods to interact with my students?

When choosing which instructional method to use, it really comes down to a number of important things to consider. First, you need to match your instructional method with each desired student learning objective (SLO; more on this in Chapters 2 and 5). For example, if you have a course SLO that requires students to do a group project, the logical choice of instruction methods is a combination of cooperative learning and project- or problem-based learning. This is what we call backwards design (see Chapter 5 for more information). Martin et al. (2019, p. 38) state that model online teachers indicate "what . . . you expect your students to know and what . . . you expect your students to do in order to learn that and how . . . they [will] demonstrate what they've learned."

40   *Instructor-to-Student Interaction*

Box 4.2 Worked Example: How to Incorporate Different Online Instructional Methods

Collaborative Learning

- Have both synchronous and asynchronous debates.
- Have students peer grade or evaluate one another on low-stakes assignments.
- Have students create and present short video position arguments.
- Assign team projects and a space for students to work together where the instructor facilitates learning.
- Plan online field trips where students are divided into dyads or groups to seek out specific information.
- Assign homework forums where students share a space to discuss homework without the presence of the instructor.

Multi-Media Learning

- Use videos such as TEDx Talks, YouTube, etc., that are either separate or embedded within a lesson.
- Use interactive websites such as Quizlet or Kahoot! to have students self-test, create content, and gamify their learning experience.

Just-in-Time Teaching

- Have students do warm-ups, which are short assignments that students complete prior to the main lesson and are designed to prompt students to think about content prior to the lesson.
- Have students complete Goodfors, which are writing prompts that attempt to have students apply content to real-life examples. For example, what is social distancing good for?
- Have students complete puzzles, which are meant to integrate the concepts of the lesson and to conclude the lesson.

Note: Information was derived from Biasutti (2017), Martin et al. (2019), Novak (2011), and Tempelman-Kluit (2006).

Therefore, you should plan strategically and choose your instructional methods based on your SLOs and students' needs.

Second, consider how well the instructional method will meet your learners' needs (Martin et al., 2019). For instance, if you are teaching a large-section general education course (e.g., Introductory Anthropology), using a combination of collaborative learning (small group discussions) and multi-media learning

Instructor-to-Student Interaction 41

(e.g., Stephen DeBerry's *Why the "Wrong Side of the Tracks" is Usually the East Side of Cities* TEDx Talk) with some just-in-time Teaching may be more effective than using direct instruction. In Martin and colleagues' (2019, p. 39) study of model online teachers, one teacher sums it up perfectly:

> In our graduate program 98% of our students work full-time and study part-time. So they really are very busy people and you really need to be careful how you lay out the course for them. . . . So it depends on your student population, if they're undergrad, if they're resident, not working full time then you may you know design it or lay it out for them a little bit differently.

In other words, adapting your online instructional methods is dependent on your students, not solely on you.

> **#MoTs use different instructional strategies based on their students' needs and their students' learning objectives.**

Practice Effective Online Teaching Skills

So far in this chapter, we have discussed how you can interact with your students through the syllabus and which instructional methods you may choose, and for the most part, this seems like a fairly straightforward process, almost like a recipe: Add all the ingredients, bake for 16 weeks, and voila! But there is more to becoming a model online teacher than that; it takes a set of specific teaching skills to succeed in the online environment (Schmidt et al., 2013). So what are these mysterious online teaching skills? Model online teachers are tech savvy, engaging, caring, flexible/open-minded, supportive, professional, and have strong communication skills that lead to greater rapport with their students (Keeley et al., 2006; Wilson et al., 2010). But how do you accomplish learning and developing these skills? It starts with a baseline assessment. Thus, how often do you:

- Praise students for their good work?
- Help students in need?
- Know your students' names?

According to Keeley and colleagues (2006), if your answer is often, you practice the teaching skill of caring. Let's try again. How often do you:

- Initiate conversation with students?
- Respond respectfully and swiftly to students' communications and comments?

42 *Instructor-to-Student Interaction*

If you responded not very often, then Keeley and colleagues would suggest that you need to work on your approachability, personability, and accessibility skills. How often would you say you:

- Meet outside of office hours?
- Accept criticism from students?
- Allow students an opportunity to make up work?
- Don't make spelling errors or mistakes, or are generally sloppy in your lessons?

If you are able to respond often, then you possess the teaching skills of being flexible/open-minded and professional (Keeley et al., 2006).

Now that you have self-assessed some of your online teaching skills, how can you improve upon these skills? One way to improve the teaching skill of professionalism is to be organized. Instructors may think that students are not aware of how unorganized they are because of the anonymity of online learning. However, THEY ARE! They can tell by whether the syllabus is complete. Or whether each module for the entire semester is not ready for prime time. Or if the instructor tends to be the stereotype of an "absent-minded professor." Another way to improve your professionalism skill is to respond to students swiftly. Now, as our significant others would say, "Don't live on email!" However, you do not need to live on email to give students prompt answers to their questions. Lead by example, meaning if you are professional and provide a mental model for students to follow, then often they will.

How do you hone your engaging teaching skills? Think of your favorite teacher of all time. What was it that they did? Likely, they were incredibly engaging, but how? According to Miller and colleagues (2011, p. 2), student engagement is the "willingness to actively participate in the learning process and persist despite obstacles and challenges." Moreover, students indicate that they are engaged with the instructor primarily through interactive lessons, informal chats and discussions, conversations through email, and feedback on assignments (Dixson, 2010). Therefore, we offer several suggestions on how to be an engaging online teacher.

First, evidence suggests that you should infuse diversity into the course by using diverse examples and discussing diversity issues (Richmond et al., 2016). Whether you use names from varied ethnicities in your assessments, or talk about current events, or ask students to share personal stories via synchronous discussions, when you do so, students will be more engaged. Second, create an active learning culture in your class (Zepke & Leach, 2010). Learning is not a spectator sport. Engage students in debates, discussions, demonstrations, and whatever other activities professionals in your field do. Third, and this is sometimes difficult, when possible allow for some synchronous interactions. Hold live Q&A sessions three to four times during the term. Hold a live study session for an exam. Have a guest speaker come in and moderate the session. Hold a wrap-up session at the end of major units that allows you to explain difficult concepts or demonstrate specific skills (Hew, 2015; Khan et al., 2017). In the end, the more you hone your engagement skills, the closer you are to becoming a model online teacher.

> **#MoTs are tech savvy, engaging, caring, flexible/open-minded, supportive, professional, and have strong communication skills that lead to great rapport.**

Finally, as likely the most daunting skill to improve upon and learn: HOW DO I IMPROVE MY TECH SKILLS?! As we all know, this is an ever-moving target. Sometimes it is difficult to keep up with the most current LMSs, video conferencing apps (e.g., Zoom), screen recording apps (e.g., Loom), anonymous texting apps (e.g., Google Voice), self-testing apps (e.g., Quizlet), synchronous polling apps (e.g., Kahoot!), microlearning apps (i.e., Digital Badges), and on and on. No, the irony is not lost on us that some of the things we just mentioned may be outdated by the time this book goes to print. This is why we suggest that you embrace technology. You don't have to be a technocrat, but you do have to constantly learn and evolve. Some of the best ways to do this is to stand on the shoulders of others, meaning use your campus teaching center, faculty development office, or educational technology staff to learn about new technological innovations to incorporate into your course. Read some of the professional periodicals such as *Inside Higher Education, The Tech Advocate*, or *Faculty Focus* to get new ideas. The point is, try not to get overwhelmed; take baby steps by introducing one piece of educational technology per term, but strive to stay informed.

Now that you have begun to learn about various teaching skills, one of the most important online teaching skills that model teachers do every day is build, establish, and maintain rapport with their students. Rapport has been widely studied and can be generally defined "as a relationship of mutual trust and liking" (Wilson et al., 2010, pp. 247–248). It is the interpersonal connection between you and your students. Wilson and Ryan (2013) state that rapport includes perceptions of the teacher (e.g., enthusiastic, receptive, reliable, caring) and elements of student engagement (e.g., likability, enjoyment, immediacy, and encouragement).

Logically, then, how do you do this? Throughout the annals of research on online education, there have been several suggestions on how to improve rapport. Allow students freedom to make choices (i.e., give them some control over their learning) about how to achieve their desired course goals (Zepke & Leach, 2010). For instance, allow students to choose among various assignments or only include their best ten out of 12 quiz scores or three out of five discussion forums. Increasing teacher and student interaction by being present in the course is paramount. Not only do you need to increase formal interaction with students (e.g.,

44 *Instructor-to-Student Interaction*

Box 4.3 Working Smarter: Online Rapport—Tricks of the Trade!

- At the start of the term, send an email that contains a video or a link to a video that welcomes your students to the class. Let your personality come out in this video.
- Throughout the course, share tidbits about yourself. Be self-deprecating and human.
- Model enthusiasm for the course content and teaching.
- Don't bluff, and be true to your word.
- Hold synchronous events (e.g., online office hours).
- Reduce barriers by avoiding formal and threatening language.
- Communicate non-course-related material (e.g., send out job ads).
- Learn something about your students (e.g., where they are from).
- The first discussion forum should be an introduction process among the students. Ask them what they do for fun and be sure to respond, in a meaningful way, to each student's response.
- Allow students to "revise and resubmit" their work for a partial increase in a grade.
- Check their progress and communicate to them that you care and are concerned.
- Use students' knowledge of technology to have them teach you about technology; it empowers them.

Note: These best practices are selected and adapted from Bain (2004), Glazier (2016), Meyers (2009), and Sull (2014).

---

discussing course content, academic advising), but you should also increase informal interactions (e.g., discussing nonacademic topics through synchronous chats and discussion forums). Additionally, be online a lot during the first part of the semester. Be visible to students. Let students know that you are there (Martin et al., 2019). These are just a couple of ideas; however, in Box 4.3, there are several other ways in which you can increase your rapport with your students.

The Great Debate: Do Model Online Teachers use Synchronous or Asynchronous Learning?

One of the most often debated dilemmas in online teaching is whether you should have synchronous or asynchronous learning. Do you have a set time where all or part of the class meets (synchronous), or should it just be when students have the time to do it (asynchronous)? Just like any educational debate, there are no winners. Rather, both synchronous and asynchronous learning have their merits

Box 4.4 Working Smarter: When and Where to Use Synchronous vs. Asynchronous Learning

Synchronous	*Asynchronous*
• Live debates • Q&A sessions • Flexible office hours that are offered at various times • Live reviews • Email or messaging communication • Live lessons • Small group discussions using messaging or video apps	• Discussion forums available for a limited amount of time • Email class information • Announcements for due dates and other class events • Short lessons that are video recorded • Peer audio or video feedback • Assessments and assignments

(Watts, 2016). In other words, there is a time and place to use each type. For instance, using synchronous chats to discuss problems with students is very effective, quick, and also develops rapport with your students (Watts, 2016). In contrast, using asynchronous discussions to present ideas and get feedback may also prove to effective (Duncan et al., 2012). There are advantages to using both. For asynchronous learning, it is flexible, allowing students to pace themselves on their own schedules, and for synchronous learning, it is engaging, builds rapport with your students, and you can discover unanticipated issues or problems.

Yet, both synchronous and asynchronous learning also have disadvantages. For synchronous learning, it often requires a rigid schedule that your students cannot adhere to, and technical difficulties sometimes get in the way (e.g., Internet speed, lack of a webcam). However, asynchronous learning may cause students to feel isolated, fall behind, give up, and perform poorly. Ultimately, when deciding what to use, the most important factor is your students. Many students enroll in online courses because of the flexibility of time; thus, keeping your students in mind and how a synchronous session may affect them is important. Box 4.4 illustrates that there are certain activities that are better suited for either synchronous or asynchronous interactions with students. As Johnson (2006) put it, both synchronous and asynchronous learning should be used to maximize student learning.

Interact With Students Via Student Evaluations of Teaching

You may not view how you evaluate your own teaching as a typical mode of interacting with your students, but it may be one of the more impactful interactions you have. Consider these two questions:

1. Do you regularly solicit summative feedback from students?
2. Do you regularly solicit formative feedback from students?

46 *Instructor-to-Student Interaction*

How did you answer? If you answered YES, that is great. If you answered NO, then there is always room for improvement. But the important question then becomes: Do you share these results with your students?

Model online teachers will collect evaluations of their teaching multiple times over the course of the semester. For instance, they may assess students' rapport and engagement at the beginning of the semester, at midterm, and at end of the semester (for more detail on student evaluations of teaching, see Chapter 5). They may do this using an online survey tool (e.g., Survey Monkey, Google Forms), conducting synchronous or asynchronous focus groups, or through focused listening (e.g., at the end of lesson collect written or audio lists of important concepts from students and review their answers at the start of the next lesson). Model online teachers collect student opinions on simple matters, such as how an assignment went or how hard a test was. But they go beyond just collecting and considering these evaluations. Model online teachers share the results of these evaluations (anonymously of course) with their students to try and improve their teaching during the term. For example, you may observe that your rapport with students is not as strong as you'd like, so you ask your students how you may improve. Or, you find through your evaluations that students feel that their voice is not being heard, so you have a synchronous discussion with your students about how to remedy the situation. The moral of the story is that model online teachers constantly collect data on their teaching effectiveness, share this data with their students while they are still teaching them, then discuss with their students how to improve their teaching and the students' learning experience.

Interact With Students Through Student Feedback

How do you give feedback on assignments and assessments to your online students? Do you write in the comment boxes within the LMS? Do you send them an email? Do you do nothing (please don't say "yes")? These methods are good asynchronous methods to provide feedback on coursework to your students, but another way you can interact with your students is through video and audio feedback (see Chapter 5 for more on evaluating students and providing feedback). By using either audio or video feedback, you will increase rapport with your students because they will feel that you are more present and caring; it may even lead to better retention of content (Ice et al., 2007). A common retort is, "I don't have time to give video or audio feedback to my students!" We suggest that you work smarter by streamlining comments using audio or video. Some LMSs allow instructors to insert audio or video messages in the same places they can provide written feedback, or you may use third-party apps (e.g., Loom, Screencast, or Snagit). Box 4.5 illustrates that some simple tricks to expedite this process. We promise you, with a little practice, providing feedback using short clips will be easier for you and more engaging for your students.

Box 4.5 Working Smarter: Let Them See and Hear You

- Create a script; keep a file of your general comments, common errors on assignments, and typical feedback to students. This will allow your feedback to be polished and reduce the "umms."
- Keep it short and conversational.
- Do not worry about production value.
- Screenshot students' assignments while you record; this allows you to specifically address their work.
- Keep your comments brief and concise; allow students to see and hear who you are as a person.
- Keep a library of these comments; you often observe the same issues/errors over and over, so you can just upload your feedback without having to create new notes.

#MoTs discuss student evaluations of their teaching and use video and chat feedback on assignments and assessments.

Stop, Think, Reflect: The Model Online Teaching Checklist for Instructor-to-Student Interaction

Ok, ok: This was a lot of information. However, the takeaway is that like all great teachers, constantly evolving your teaching is what will make you better. In order to improve your interaction with your students, you have to be proactive. Don't let the semester just fly by without actively engaging with your students (whether synchronously or asynchronously). We want you to go through the checklist that follows and identify the areas in which you are excelling and in which you need improvement. Then set a plan to increase interactions with your online students.

- ☐ Your syllabus communicates who you are as a teacher.
- ☐ Your syllabus reflects effective use of online pedagogy.
- ☐ Your syllabus communicates all the ways students can contact you and when.
- ☐ Your syllabus sets a positive tone for the course (e.g., uses positive and rewarding language).
- ☐ Your syllabus is written in the first person with proper pronoun use.
- ☐ You use multiple instructional methods.
- ☐ You adapt your instruction based on student needs and learning objectives.

48   *Instructor-to-Student Interaction*

- ☐ You strive to be a better online teacher.
- ☐ You are enthusiastic when you teach online.
- ☐ You are happy, positive, and humorous online.
- ☐ You are professional.
- ☐ You understand your online students.
- ☐ You encourage your online students.
- ☐ You care about your online students.
- ☐ You are approachable online through multiple forms of communication.
- ☐ You are compassionate, open-minded, and flexible with your online students.
- ☐ You provide written, audio, and video feedback to your students.
- ☐ You discuss your current and past student evaluations of teaching with your students.

Tips for Continued Learning About Online Instructor-to-Student Interaction

- Grab Germano and Nicholls' *Syllabus: The Remarkable, Remarkable, Unremarkable Document That Changes Everything* (2020) to learn more about how to improve your syllabus.
- For different instructional strategies and developing the syllabus, check out Ko and Rossen's (2017) *Teaching Online: A Practical Guide.*
- Although originally designed for K–12 education, Ferriter and Cancellieri's (2016) book on *Creating a Culture of Feedback* provides some very innovative ways in which you can use feedback mechanisms to interact with your students.

5 Online Assessment

The current watchword on Guy's campus, and many others in higher education, is student retention. With the number of high school graduates in his state dwindling, competition for students is fierce. As part of retention efforts, Guy's administration asks teachers to consider the performance of every student in every class and submit an "early alert" report for any student who is struggling in the first two weeks. For instructors who design courses around the traditional midterm and final exam, such early alerts are a baffling impossibility. For online instructors, early alerts simply ask them to report one of the many assessments built into their course design.

Consider the information Guy has about students two weeks into his online course: He knows the exact dates and times students have logged into the LMS, as well as how much time they have spent on the course pages. Every contribution to discussion is saved and tabulated for later review. He can also examine if they have submitted reading assignments, the rubric scores they received, and any comments he left on their work. Forget about the first two weeks of class, he could complete an early alert after the first two days. Model online teachers design courses so that they take advantage of online assessment opportunities and the information they produce about student learning and performance.

How to Adapt Assessment to Online Instruction

Imagine if there was a magical teaching tool that could solve your pedagogical problems. What would it do? Here is our list: Motivate students to complete learning tasks, improve student learning, reduce student confusion about assignments, increase student satisfaction with our teaching, and prove the value of our pedagogy to others. If those outcomes sound as good to you as they do to us, then you should be invested in the not-so-magical process of assessment.

The term "assessment" refers to many things in higher education, which can lead to confusion. Educators often use assessment as a blanket term for all methods used to evaluate student learning, such as tests, papers, and presentations. Others use assessment as a synonym for "collecting data from students," whatever that data may be. Assessment also refers to the bureaucratic procedures

50　*Online Assessment*

associated with reporting learning outcomes for the purpose of accreditation. These are all types of assessment, but for model online teachers, assessment refers to a process of learning-focused planning, checking, and revising that is integral to course design and implementation.

This chapter will outline model online teaching practices related to the assessment of student learning and the evaluation of teachers. The assessment process as it relates to student learning is a core component of online course design, evaluation, and improvement. Model online teachers set learning goals, select methods to evaluate students' achievement of those goals, plan educational activities to help students reach the goals, and use evidence of learning to provide feedback and make improvements. The process of evaluating teachers parallels assessment of student learning but emphasizes the use of student feedback to improve instruction. Model online teachers regularly ask students for feedback and use it to guide adjustments to instruction and course design (see Chapter 4 on how online teachers accomplish this task). Using these assessment processes, model online teachers can provide evidence that learning occurs in their courses and that students are satisfied with that learning—this is consequential information in the context of a higher education culture still rife with skepticism about the effectiveness of online learning.

The Process of Assessing Student Learning Online

Assessment is essential to model teaching in any format, but there is no way for an online course to be effective without skillful implementation of the assessment process. If you reflect on the in-person courses that you have taken or observed, there are probably some teachers who made up for sloppy course design by being dynamos in the classroom. Although there are ways to be a dynamo in online courses (see Chapter 4), there is no making up for an online course that lacks direction, meaningful assignments, or useful feedback. For online courses, the assessment process is synonymous with effective course design. Model online teachers engage in that assessment process by doing the following.

- Defining and communicating learning objectives
- Aligning course activities with learning objectives
- Providing feedback to students based on their achievement of learning objectives
- Using evaluations of student learning to inform course improvements

Communicating Learning Objectives

People need guides to find their way in new environments. Imagine a traveler who is dropped off in a large foreign city and told that they have to catch a bus in the city's central plaza if they want to get back to their hotel. A combination of luck and strategic tailing of buses might lead to the traveler to the plaza,

Online Assessment 51

but the trek would be easier with a clearly labeled map. It would also be more enjoyable. Freed up from the confusion of being lost, the traveler could take in the atmosphere of interesting new buildings, neighborhoods, and people. Students are like travelers in an academic discipline that is foreign to them—they need a guide. In online courses, learning objectives are an essential guide for students.

> #MoTs communicate specific, measurable learning objectives in their syllabus and other course materials.

Model online teachers plan courses using backwards design. What makes the course design "backward" is that it starts with the product of education—what students learn. Thus, the first step for teachers designing an online course is to write specific, measurable learning objectives that define what students should be able to do after they complete the course (see Box 5.1). After defining what should be learned, the next step is to plan the assignments students will complete to demonstrate that they have achieved the learning objectives. Only in the final step do teachers create the activities that students will complete to help them achieve the learning objectives.

For learning objectives to benefit students, teachers must clearly communicate them throughout online course materials. Teachers can use many LMS tools to convey objectives. The most common method would be to have written instructions prominently placed at the start of each module on the LMS. Teachers might even use the features of their LMS to require students to check off the objectives as a prerequisite to releasing the rest of the module's content. Of course, teachers can provide the same content using audio or video messages. Another way to introduce learning objectives is send them via email or the LMS announcement function as part of a message to students at the start of each new module. Finally, each course assignment includes instructions, and they are another place to list objectives so that the ultimate learning goal of the assignment is just as clear to students as the expectations for content, format, and submission.

Alignment of Learning Objectives, Assignments, and Activities

In backwards design, learning objectives guide all course activities. What students do to learn and the ways they demonstrate learning must be aligned with the learning objectives. Consider this all-too-common example of bad alignment. An instructor sets the goal for students to "think critically about course topics," but the learning activities include watching lecture videos, taking multiple-choice quizzes on facts from the lectures, and a cumulative final exam made up of old quiz questions. How is critical thinking learned? And where is it demonstrated? To be consistent with model teaching practices, the instructor needs to add learning activities that promote critical thinking and a method for

52 *Online Assessment*

Box 5.1 Worked Example: The ABCs of Writing Learning Objectives

Writing learning objectives is as easy as **A**-**B**-**C**.

- **A**udience—Who will be learning?
- **B**ehavior—What will they learn?
- **C**ondition—Under what conditions will they demonstrate learning?

Here is an example of a learning objective in ABC format:

- Students in English Composition (A) will recognize professional vs. unprofessional tone (B) when editing their own writing (C).

After writing an objective, evaluate it according the following standards:

- Is the objective a measurable behavior?
- Does the objective represent meaningful learning?
- Does the objective focus on what students will achieve (e.g., evaluate theories) rather than instructional methods (e.g., read a book)?
- Can achievement of the objective be reasonably evaluated using course assignments?

---

evaluating the outcome of those activities. For example, students might analyze and evaluate course material on a discussion board and then write an essay that the instructor scores using a critical thinking rubric. Model online teachers align all learning activities and evaluations of learning with learning objectives.

#MoTs align course assignments and activities with learning objectives.

The process of assessment is continuous in online courses (Stavredes, 2011). In-person courses have traditionally followed a pattern of frequent lectures punctuated with high-stakes exams. Consequently, there are only a few points in the term when teachers know how well students are learning course material. In contrast, online courses consist of an ongoing series of learning activities and assignments that continually assess student learning. In a very real sense, the assessment process in online courses is "the class."

Graded assignments in online courses are more than summative evaluations of learning; they are learning tools. For an in-person course, weeks might go by without a graded assignment, but in online courses, assignments start from the first day and continue with regularity—typically multiple assignments per week—for the entire term (Conrad & Openo, 2018; Darby & Lang, 2019). The rapidity of assignments means that students are constantly engaged with course material and constantly receiving feedback that helps them learn.

Assignments can also serve as scaffolding toward the achievement of major learning objectives. Consider a course with an objective for students to apply theory to a case study during a collaborative presentation. Students must first learn the basic skills needed to work toward that goal. For example, students might post on a group discussion board to learn how to use LMS collaboration tools, take a quiz to learn a theory, write an essay to learn how to apply the theory, and create a PowerPoint slide with narration to learn how to make an oral presentation. At each step, the assignment would include instructions and an explanation of how the assignment relates to course learning objectives. In addition, at every step the teacher could use students' performance on the assignments as an indicator of their progress toward the learning objective.

When aligning learning objectives, online teachers should also ensure that the objectives are meaningful. Students will skip supplemental activities and ungraded assignments with ruthless efficiency. As such, make assignments meaningful to students by indicating their status as required or optional. In addition, make required assignments count for something in the gradebook, even if the impact on final grades is trivial. Teachers should also remember that high-stakes, single-shot assignments lose some of their meaningfulness in online courses. Final papers that students complete in one draft without connection to prior assignments could encourage slapdash work or even plagiarism because students fail to see the point. Scaffolded assignments should lead up to final papers and make its purpose obvious to students.

In an early foray into online teaching, Guy included a test question that asked students to summarize the methods and results of a famous study. One student simply cut and pasted the study's abstract as their answer. What could he do? That was the best summary possible. He learned from that experience that teachers must also make tests meaningful in the online context. Major tests that students complete under time pressure could encourage cheating. Switching to open-book tests with extended time is an alternative, but such tests are better aligned with learning objectives that require application, analysis, or evaluation rather than reproduction of facts. To illustrate, evaluating achievement of the learning objective "summarize the standards of professional ethics" would be useless on an open-book test because students could simply copy the standards, whereas the learning objective "evaluate the ethics of real-world professional actions" forces students to understand and apply the standards—it is also more meaningful.

Providing Constructive Feedback Online

Returning to the example of a traveler trying to catch a bus at the central plaza of a foreign city, giving them a map would be a good start in helping them find

54   *Online Assessment*

their way, but a smartphone app that provided step-by-step instructions would be even better. Such an app offers more than directions. It corrects wrong turns. Translating this example to teaching online, learning objectives are a good start in directing student learning, but the teacher must also provide feedback that corrects students' efforts at learning when it goes off track. Giving feedback on student work is one of the essential forms of student–teacher contact in online courses (see Chapters 3 and 4). However, feedback must consist of more than assigning summative grades; it should also include formative evaluations that help students progress toward learning objectives.

> **#MoTs provide constructive feedback to students that relates to their achievement of learning objectives.**

Model online teachers provide ongoing feedback to students in online classes. Compared to the traditional four exams and a term paper approach of in-person courses, the number of assignments to grade in online courses can be alarming. An average weekly module might include a quiz, multiple discussion board forums, and an assignment related to an ongoing project. Moreover, this pattern repeats week after week throughout the term. Despite this apparent glut of grading, model online teachers use technology to efficiently provide students with quick and useful feedback.

The technology inherent to online courses streamlines the process of providing students with feedback (Heinrich et al., 2009; Hepplestone et al., 2011). Correction of written assignments can occur quickly and reliably using the comment and mark-up features of the LMS or word processing programs. Teachers can provide detailed feedback because typing comments is easy and frequently used comments can be saved for later coping and pasting onto other students' work. Online feedback also benefits from the use of rubrics. Integration of rubrics into a course LMS is seamless, and completed rubrics are automatically and permanently attached to assignments. Ratings on rubrics can even produce specific feedback informing the student how they can improve (see Chapter 3, Box 3.3 for a rubric example). Once saved on the LMS, students can access feedback immediately—no more waiting to hand back papers in class. See Chapter 4, Box 4.5 on how to engage students through written, audio, and video feedback.

The advantages of providing feedback online are compounded for tests and quizzes. Correction of multiple-choice and fill-in-the-black questions can be automated in the LMS. Because the process is automated, allowing students to repeatedly take quizzes until mastery requires the same amount of work as allowing them a single attempt. Going beyond simple feedback that answers are right or wrong, specific student responses to questions can prompt automated messages. For example, a wrong answer might prompt students to receive a reminder about resources to help them learn the relevant material. Once again, students do not need to wait for teachers to correct their answers; feedback can be available to students the second after they respond.

Discussion boards are a core learning tool in online courses (see Chapter 3), and they too provide some feedback advantages over in-person courses. Unlike in-person discussions that are difficult to observe and evaluate as they occur synchronously in real-time, the asynchronous discussions that occur in online courses allow teachers a direct view into every students' attempt to engage intellectually with course materials. Having a complete record of students' online posts gives teachers the option to evaluate discussions in detail, offering correction or reinforcement as needed. By setting expectations for discussion and grading participation with a rubric (see Chapter 3), teachers can also provide swift feedback to students about the appropriateness and adequacy of their contributions.

Teachers can use the course LMS to provide feedback based on a snapshot of student activity in the course. LMS student performance dashboards provide information about, quite literally, everything students do in the system. To get an objective snapshot of student engagement in the course, teachers can examine metrics such as frequency of student log ins, time spent on the LMS, number of assignments submitted, and number of discussion board posts. When levels of student engagement fall below an acceptable level, the teacher can send emails and alerts, often automatically (see Box 5.2), to check in with students and to encourage a change in behavior.

Box 5.2 Working Smarter: Using LMS Automatization

Instructor presence in the course is essential part of model teaching online. Many aspects of being present in the course, such as commenting on discussion boards or completing rubrics, require timely work by the instructor. However, other signs of instructor presence can also be automated in the LMS to minimize work for the instructor but still indicate their presence to students. Here are some of the typical LMS automatization features.

- Course-wide announcements
- Messages when students have not logged into the system
- Reminders for assignment due dates
- Recognition for completing tasks
- Grading of quizzes
- Personalized feedback for quiz responses
- Messages when students' grades reach a certain level

56 *Online Assessment*

Making Assessment-Based Changes

Assessment is a process: Plan, check, revise, repeat. Model online teachers continuously engage in this process by gathering information about student learning and determining if students are adequately achieving course learning objectives. If they are not, then changes can occur to syllabi, lesson plans, assignments, and any other course materials. If learning objectives are properly aligned with assignments, then teachers will automatically have information they can use to make changes to improve student outcomes in the current course and future courses.

> **#MoTs change online course materials or methods based on formal and informal assessment.**

Course design and the assessment processes are one and the same for online courses. Everything is visible in online courses—every assignment, every discussion post, every click. Based on this and other rich data from the LMS, online teachers have the ability to not only adjust from semester to semester but also to adjust from module to module. Model online teachers do not wait for a major paper or exam to find out if students are completing coursework and understanding material. From the first day of class, teachers can monitor access to the LMS and required materials. Have students not logged on to the LMS? Deadlines may be reemphasized. Are quiz scores low? Students might need clearer guidelines on what is important in the readings. Do rubric scores on an assignment suggest misunderstanding of the task? An example assignment might be needed. Are discussion board posts consistently off topic? Clearer expectations for the substance of posts might focus the discussions. As these examples illustrate, model online teachers use the information available to them on the LMS to make midcourse adjustments.

Teaching Effectiveness Assessment Process

Once more, consider that traveler trying to catch a bus in a foreign city. A map would help. A smartphone app that gave course corrections would help even more. But what if the app was difficult to install? What if the app's instructions were confusing? Or, what if app's course corrections were insulting? "Your *other* right, idiot!" To make improvements, the designer could ask users for feedback about their experiences with the app. Anyone who has written or read a product review online should understand the value of encouraging students to provide feedback on teaching.

Both students and teachers require feedback. Students need teachers to tell them if their attempts at learning have been successful, and teachers need students to tell them if their attempts at education have been successful (at least in one sense). The process of assessing student learning provides teachers with the most important feedback about educational success—achievement of learning objectives—but model online teachers also consider students' perceptions of their educational experience. After all, students have unique a perspective on the functioning of courses, and the best teachers design courses that students see as both valuable and enjoyable.

Chapter 4 outlined the importance of communicating with students by asking for feedback. Gathering feedback, although an important part of student-teacher contact, does not lead to improvement on its own. Model online teachers use feedback as part of a multistep, improvement-focused assessment process. First, they solicit formal and informal feedback from students. Second, they set specific, attainable goals for improvement based on that feedback, ideally in consultation with a pedagogical expert. Third, they change instructional methods or materials to reach their goal. Finally, they ask students for feedback again.

> **#MoTs set goals for the improvement of teaching based on student feedback and incorporate this feedback to revise their course and change instructional methods.**

The process of setting goals and making changes based on student feedback is the same across course formats, so the key question for online teachers is if the definition of good teaching, and its evaluation, is the same across course formats. In fact, experts argue that evaluation of in-person and online courses have more similarities than differences (Benton & Cashin, 2012; Drouin, 2012). Unsurprisingly, ratings of effective technology use is the main difference between in-person and online student evaluations (online teachers receive better evaluations, by the way).

Despite the overlap in model online and in-person teaching, the evaluation of online teaching has some unique challenges (Berk, 2013; Tobin et al., 2015). If student evaluation surveys are out of date or poorly designed, they may have items that are irrelevant or inappropriate for online courses. In addition, the evaluation of online courses needs to account for the general absence of "classes," both in the sense of synchronous meeting periods and physical meeting places. Moreover, online courses weave together instruction, course design, and technology in ways that are difficult to separate. For example, a negative evaluation of online discussion boards could result from neglectful moderation (instructor), irrelevant topics (design), or a clunky interface (technology). Similarly, online courses are often based on predesigned templates, but most student evaluation surveys include questions about instruction and design. Overall, online teachers should exercise some caution when interpreting student evaluation feedback taken from surveys designed for traditional in-person courses.

For teachers whose institutions have not adopted online-friendly student evaluation surveys, there are some practical solutions to obtaining meaningful feedback. Many institutions allow teachers or departments to add personalized items

58 *Online Assessment*

to student evaluation surveys, and online teachers could lobby for the inclusion of relevant items. Of course, every LMS includes a student survey function that instructors can use to obtain the exact feedback they need at any point in the term. When selecting student evaluation surveys for online courses, it is best to use published measures with established validity, of which there are many (for suggestions see Berk, 2013; Drouin, 2012). However, obtaining precise feedback sometimes requires the writing of new survey items (see Box 5.3).

In the online education world, discussion of teacher evaluation is incomplete without mentioning rubrics and checklists. Unlike their in-person counterparts, online courses often go through certification to ensure basic quality. These certifications typically involve rubrics or checklists that evaluators use

---

Box 5.3 Worked Example: Writing Student Evaluation Items

One method for evaluating online teaching is to follow Chickering and Gamson's seven principles for good practice in higher education (Tobin et al., 2015). Ask students if the course and instruction are consistent with the principles.

Principle of good practice	*Possible student evaluation topics*
Student-faculty contact	• Course announcements • Online office hours • Synchronous meetings • Responsiveness on discussion boards
Student-student cooperation	• Group project management • Discussion board management • Usefulness of peer feedback
Emphasizing active learning	• Value of discussion • Value of projects • Value of quizzes
Maximizing time on task	• Amount of time spent on class • Connection of learning objectives to class work • Use of optional course material
Setting high expectations	• Course difficulty • Clarity of time needed on assignments • Expectations for learning and success
Providing prompt feedback	• Personal responses made on discussion boards • Feedback kept up with modules • Use of LMS to provide immediate feedback
Respecting diversity in learning	• Presented course information using text and media • Helped students from varied backgrounds understand • Ease of learning material

to determine if the course meets standard design criteria. The most prominent example is Quality Matters certification (www.qualitymatters.org), but others include the SUNY Online Course Quality Review (https://oscqr.suny.edu) and the Illinois Online Network Quality Online Course Initiative (www.uis.edu/ion). For model online teachers, having outside certification based one or more of these evaluations is a respected sign of quality. However, teachers can also use the standards from these evaluations for formative feedback. For example, they could ask students to consider the course in relation to the standards, ask for a peer review, or conduct a self-evaluation. No matter who the course evaluator is, these rubrics and checklists will provide useful information for goal setting and course improvement.

Stop, Think, Reflect: The Model Online Teaching Checklist for Online Assessment

Plan, check, revise, repeat—this is how online assessment works. For assessment student learning, model online teachers set learning objectives, share them with students, determine how successfully students have met those objectives, and then make plans to improve that success. Along the way they provide students with useful feedback on their progress toward achieving the objectives. Model online teachers also engage in a parallel process of assessing their own success in meeting students' learning needs. This book works the same way. Take some time to reflect on your teaching and how consistent it is with the characteristics of model teaching outlined in this chapter. Then, set goals that move you toward greater consistency.

- ☐ Communicate learning objectives in syllabi.
- ☐ Display learning objectives in LMS modules.
- ☐ Provide learning objectives for assignments.
- ☐ Align online course assignments and activities with learning objectives.
- ☐ Assign work throughout the course that moves students toward the achievement of learning objectives.
- ☐ Provide frequent feedback to students about their achievement of learning objectives.
- ☐ Scaffold assignments to allow students to achieve complex learning objectives.
- ☐ Use LMS technology to monitor student work and progress toward achievement of learning objectives.
- ☐ Use LMS technology to provide timely feedback on achievement of learning objectives.
- ☐ Change online course materials or methods based on assessment results during the term and from term to term.
- ☐ Set goals for the improvement of teaching based on student feedback.
- ☐ Incorporate student feedback into course revisions and changes to instructional methods.

Tips for Continued Learning About Online Assessment

- Conrad and Openo's (2018) book *Assessment Strategies for Online Learning: Engagement and Authenticity* provides a guide for how to make assessment an essential and meaningful part of online courses.
- Drouin's (2012) e-book chapter "What's the Story on Evaluations of Online Teaching?" discusses the issues to consider when using student evaluations in online teaching.
- The National Institution for Learning Outcomes Assessment (NILOA) has a website full of excellent assessment information, and it includes resources specific for online teaching: www.learningoutcomesassessment.org/.

References

American Psychological Association. (2013). *APA guidelines for the undergraduate psychology major Version 2.0.* American Psychological Association.

Anderson, L. W., Krathwohl, D. R., Airasian, P. W., Cruikshank, K. A., Mayer, R. E., Pintrich, P. R., Raths, J., & Wittrock, M. C. (Eds.). (2001). *A taxonomy for learning, teaching, and assessing: A revision of Bloom's taxonomy of educational objectives.* Longman.

Angelo, T. A., & Cross, K. P. (1993). *Classroom assessment techniques: A handbook for college teachers* (2 ed.). Jossey-Bass.

Association of American Colleges and Universities. (n.d.). *Essential learning outcomes.* Retrieved from www.aacu.org/essential-learning-outcomes

Bain, K. (2004). *What the best college teachers do.* Harvard University Press.

Bart, M. (2011). Fostering student interaction in the online classroom. *Faculty Focus.* Retrieved from https://www.facultyfocus.com/articles/online-education/fostering-student-interaction-in-the-online-classroom/

Benassi, V. A., Overson, C. E., & Hakala, C. M. (2014). *Applying science of learning in education: Infusing psychological science into the curriculum.* Retrieved from http://teachpsych.org/ebooks/asle2014/index.php

Benton, S. L., & Cashin, W. E. (2012). *Student ratings of teaching: A summary of research and literature.* The IDEA Center.

Berk, R. A. (2013). Face-to-face versus online course evaluations: A "Consumer's Guide" to seven strategies. *Journal of Online Learning & Teaching, 9*(1), 140–148.

Biasutti, M. (2017). A comparative analysis of forums and wikis as tools for online collaborative learning. *Computers & Education, 111*, 158–171. https://doi.org/10.1016/j.compedu.2017.04.006

Boysen, G. A., Richmond, A. S., & Gurung, R. A. R. (2015). Model teaching criteria for psychology: Initial documentation of teachers' self-reported competency. *Scholarship of Teaching and Learning in Psychology, 1*(1), 48–59. http://dx.doi.org/10.1037/stl0000023

Bransford, J. D., Brown, A. L., & Cocking, R. R. (1999). *How people learn: Brain mind, experience, and school.* National Academy Press.

Brewer, P. E., & Brewer, E. C. (2015). Pedagogical perspectives for the online education skeptic. *Journal on Excellence in College Teaching, 26*(1), 29–52.

Chickering, A. W., & Ehrmann, S. C. (1996). Implementing the seven principles: Technology as lever. *AAHE Bulletin, 49*, 3–6.

Chickering, A. W., & Gamson, Z. F. (1987). Seven principles for good practice in undergraduate education. *AAHE Bulletin, 3*, 2–6.

Conrad, D., & Openo, J. (2018). *Assessment strategies for online learning: Engagement and authenticity.* AU Press.

62   *References*

Darby, F., & Lang, J. M. (2019). *Small teaching online: Applying learning science in online classes*. Jossey-Bass.

Davis, B. G. (2009). *Tools for teaching*. John Wiley & Sons.

Dick, W., Carey, L., & Carey, J. O. (2015). *The systemic design of instruction* (8th ed.). Pearson.

Dixson, M. D. (2010). Creating effective student engagement in online courses: What do students find engaging? *Journal of the Scholarship of Teaching and Learning*, 1–13.

Drouin, M. (2012). What's the story on evaluations of online teaching? In M. E. Kite (Ed.), *Effective evaluation of teaching: A guide for faculty and administrators* (pp. 60–70). Society for the Teaching of Psychology. Retrieved from www.teachpsych.org/Resources/Documents/ebooks/evals2012.pdf

Duncan, K., Kenworthy, A., & McNamara, R. (2012). The effect of synchronous and asynchronous participation on students' performance in online accounting courses. *Accounting Education*, *21*(4), 431–449. https://doi.org/10.1080/09639284.2012.673387

Ferriter, W. M., & Cancellieri, P. J. (2016). *Creating a culture of feedback*. Solution Tree Press.

Gannon, K. M. (2020). *Radical hope: A teaching manifesto*. West Virginia University Press.

Germano, W., & Nicholls, K. (2020). *Syllabus: The remarkable, unremarkable document that changes everything*. Princeton University Press.

Glazier, R. A. (2016). Building rapport to improve retention and success in online classes. *Journal of Political Science Education*, *12*(4), 437–456. https://doi.org/10.1080/15512169.2016.1155994

Gurung, R. A. R., & Landrum, R. E. (2015). Editorial. *Scholarship of Teaching and Learning in Psychology*, *1*(1), 1–6. https://doi.org/10.1037/stl0000026

Gurung, R. A. R., Richmond, A. S., & Boysen, G. A. (2018). Studying excellence in teaching: The story so far. In B. Buskist & J. Keeley (Eds.), *Habits and practices of master teachers: International perspectives on excellent teaching* (pp. 11–20). Wiley.

Harnish, R. J., & Bridges, K. R. (2011). Effect of syllabus tone: Students' perceptions of instructor and course. *Social Psychology of Education*, *14*(3), 319–330. https://doi.org/10.1007/s11218-011-9152-4

Heinrich, E., Milne, J., Ramsay, A., & Morrison, D. (2009). Recommendations for the use of e-tools for improvements around assignment marking quality. *Assessment & Evaluation in Higher Education*, *34*(4), 469–479. https://doi.org/10.1080/02602930802071122

Hepplestone, S., Holden, G., Irwin, B., Parkin, H. J., & Thorpe, L. (2011). Using technology to encourage student engagement with feedback: A literature review. *Research in Learning Technology*, *19*(2), 117–127. http://dx.doi.org/10.1080/21567069.2011.586677

Hew, K. F. (2015). Towards a model of engaging online students: Lessons from MOOCs and four policy documents. *International Journal of Information and Education Technology*, *5*(6), 425–435. https://doi.org/10.7763/IJIET.2015.V5.543

Homa, N., Hackathorn, J., Brown, C. M., Garczynski, A., Solomon, E. D., Tennial, R., Sanborn, U. A., & Gurung, R. A. R. (2013). An analysis of learning objectives and content coverage in introductory psychology syllabi. *Teaching of Psychology*, *40* (3), 169–174. https://doi.org/10.1177/0098628313487456

References 63

Ice, P., Curtis, R., Phillips, P., & Wells, J. (2007). Using asynchronous audio feedback to enhance teaching presence and students' sense of community. *Journal of Asynchronous Learning Networks, 11*(2), 3–25.

Johnson, G. M. (2006). Synchronous and asynchronous text-based CMC in educational contexts: A review of recent research. *TechTrends, 50*(4), 46–53. https://doi.org/10.1007/s11528-006-0046-9

Keeley, J., Smith, D., & Buskist, W. (2006). The Teacher Behavior Checklist: Factor analysis of its utility for evaluating teaching. *Teaching of Psychology, 33*(2), 84–91. https://doi.org/10.1207/s15328023top3302_1

Khan, A., Egbue, O., Palkie, B., & Madden, J. (2017). Active learning: Engaging students to maximize learning in an online course. *Electronic Journal of E-Learning, 15*(2), 107–115.

Kim, K. J., & Bonk, C. J. (2006). The future of online teaching and learning in higher education. *Educause Quarterly, 29*(4), 22–30.

Kim, Y., & Ekachai, D. G. (2020). Exploring the effects of different online syllabus formats on student engagement and course-taking intentions. *College Teaching, 68*(4), 1–11. https://doi.org/10.1080/87567555.2020.1785381

Ko, S., & Rossen, S. (2017). *Teaching online: A practical guide.* Taylor & Francis.

Kuh, G. D. (2008). *High-impact educational practices: What they are, who has access to them, and why they matter.* Association of American Colleges & Universities.

Linder, K. E., & Hayes, C. M. (2018). *High-impact practices in online education: Research and best practices.* Stylus.

Major, C. H. (2015). *Teaching online: A guide to theory, research, and practice.* Johns Hopkins University Press.

Martin, F., Ritzhaupt, A., Kumar, S., & Budhrani, K. (2019). Award-winning faculty online teaching practices: Course design, assessment and evaluation, and facilitation. *The Internet and Higher Education, 42*, 34–43. https://doi.org/10.1016/j.iheduc.2019.04.001

McCabe, M. F., & Gonzales-Flores, P. (2017). *Essentials of online teaching: A standards-based guide.* Taylor & Francis.

McKeachie, W. J., & Svinicki, M. (2012). *McKeachie's teaching tips: Strategies, research, and theory for college and university teachers* (12th ed.). Houghton Mifflin.

McKinney, K. (2018). *Enhancing learning through the scholarship of teaching and learning: The challenges and joys of juggling.* Jossey-Bass.

Meyers, S. A. (2009). Do your students care whether you care about them? *College Teaching, 57*(4), 205–210. https://doi.org/10.1080/87567550903218620

Miller, R. L., Amsel, E., Kowalewski, B. M., Beins, B. C., Keith, K. D., & Peden, B. F. (2011). *Promoting student engagement (vol 1): Programs, techniques and opportunities.* Retrieved from http://teachpsych.org/ebooks/pse2011/index.php

Nilson, L. B., & Goodson, L. A. (2018). *Online teaching at its best: Merging instructional design with teaching and learning research.* Jossey-Bass.

Novak, G. M. (2011). Just-in-time teaching. *New Directions for Teaching and Learning, 2011*(128), 63–73. https://doi.org/10.1002/tl.469

Palloff, R. M., & Pratt, K. (2007). *Building online learning communities: Effective strategies for the virtual classroom.* John Wiley & Sons.

Parker, R. E. (2013). *Redesigning courses for online delivery: Design, interaction, media & evaluation.* Emerald Group Publishing.

64 References

Parkes, J., & Harris, M. B. (2002). The purposes of a syllabus. *College Teaching, 50*(2), 55–61. https://doi.org/10.1080/87567550209595875

Persellin, D. C., & Daniels, M. B. (2014). *A concise guide to improving student learning: Six evidence-based principles and how to apply them.* Stylus.

Rao, K., Edelen-Smith, P., & Wailehua, C. U. (2015). Universal design for online courses: Applying principles to pedagogy. *Open Learning: The Journal of Open, Distance and e-Learning, 30*(1), 35–52. https://doi.org/10.1080/02680513.2014.991300

Richmond, A. S. (2016). A primer for constructing a learner-centered syllabus: One professor's journey. *IDEA,60*, 1–14. Retrieved from www.ideaedu.org/Portals/0/Uploads/Documents/IDEA%20Papers/IDEA%20Papers/PaperIDEA_60.pdf

Richmond, A. S., Boysen, G., & Gurung, R. A. R. (2016). *An evidence-based guide to college and university teaching: Developing the model teacher.* Routledge.

Richmond, A. S., Boysen, G. A., Gurung, R. A. R., Tazeau, Y. N., Meyers, S. A., & Sciutto, M. J. (2014). Aspirational model teaching criteria for psychology. *Teaching of Psychology, 41*(4), 281–295. https://doi.org/10.1177/0098628314549699

Riggs, S. (2019). *Thrive online: A new approach to building expertise and confidence as an online educator.* Stylus.

Robinson Wolf, Z., Czekanski, K. E., & Dillon, P. M. (2014). Course syllabi: Components and outcomes assessment. *Journal of Nursing Education and Practice, 4*(1), 100–107. https://doi.org/10.5430/jnep.v4n1p100

Ryan, M. (2012). Conceptualizing and teaching discursive and performative reflection in higher education. *Studies in Continuing Education, 34*(2), 207–223. https://doi.org/10.1080/0158037X.2011.611799

Schmidt, S. W., Hodge, E. M., & Tschida, C. M. (2013). How university faculty members developed their online teaching skills. *Quarterly Review of Distance Education, 14*(3), 131.

Smith, P. L., & Ragan, T. L. (2005). *Instructional design* (3rd ed.). Wiley.

Spector, J. M., Merrill, M. D., Elen, J., & Bishop, M. J. (2015). *Handbook of research on educational communications and technology.* Springer.

Stavredes, T. (2011). *Effective online teaching: Foundations and strategies.* Jossey-Bass.

Stein, D. S., & Wanstreet, C. E. (2017). *Jump-start your online classroom: Mastering five challenges in five days.* Stylus.

Stommel, J. (2020). *How to build and online learning community: 6 theses.* Retrieved from www.jessestommel.com/how-to-build-an-online-learning-community-6-theses/

Sulik, G., & Keys, J. (2014). "Many students really do not yet know how to behave!" The syllabus as a tool for socialization. *Teaching Sociology, 42*, 151–160. https://doi.org/10.1177/0092055X13513243

Sull, E. C. (2014). Student engagement, motivation, and rapport. *Distance Learning, 11*(3), 5–9.

Suskie, L. (2018). *Assessing student learning: A common sense guide.* John Wiley & Sons.

Tallent-Runnels, M. K., Thomas, J. A., Lan, W. Y., Cooper, S., Ahern, T. C., Shaw, S. M., & Liu, X. (2006). Teaching courses online: A review of the research. *Review of Educational Research, 76*(1), 93–135. https://doi.org/10.3102/00346543076001093

Tempelman-Kluit, N. (2006). Multimedia learning theories and online instruction. *College & Research Libraries, 67*(4), 364–369. https://doi.org/10.5860/crl.67.4.364

Tobin, T. J., & Behling, K. T. (2018). *Reach everyone, teach everyone: Universal design for learning in higher education.* West Virginia University Press.

Tobin, T. J., Mandernach, B. J., & Taylor, A. H. (2015). *Evaluating online teaching: Implementing best practices*. John Wiley & Sons.

Vai, M., & Sosulski, K. (2011). *Essentials of online course design: A standards-based guide*. Taylor & Francis.

Watts, L. (2016). Synchronous and asynchronous communication in distance learning: A review of the literature. *Quarterly Review of Distance Education, 17*(1), 23–32.

Wilson, J. H., & Ryan, R. G. (2013). Professor-student rapport scale six items predict student outcomes. *Teaching of Psychology, 40*(2), 130–133. https://doi.org/10.1177/0098628312475033

Wilson, J. H., Ryan, R. G., & Pugh, J. L. (2010). Professor-student rapport scale predicts student outcomes. *Teaching of Psychology, 37*(4), 246–251. https://doi.org/10.1080/00986283.2010.510976

Zepke, N., & Leach, L. (2010). Improving student engagement: Ten proposals for action. *Active Learning in Higher Education, 11*(3), 167–177. https://doi.org/10.1177/1469787410379680

Index

Note: Page numbers in *italics* indicate a figure on the corresponding page.

absent-minded professor 42
academic technology departments 3
active learning 26–27; culture in class 42; form of 39; in online courses 29
active listening 5
American Historical Association 11
American Psychological Association (APA) 11
assessment 7–8, 41, 46, 49–50; defined 49; and evaluations 5; formative 33; informal 33; student learning 11; *see also* online assessment
assignments 6, 13, 53; audio and video 19; course 51–52; feedback on 42, 46; graded 52–53; self-evaluation 29; single-shot 53
Association of American Colleges and Universities 13
asynchronous collaborative projects 32
asynchronous learning 44–45
audio and video assignments 19

backwards design 13, 39, 51
Bain, K. 36, 44
Biasutti, M. 40
Bloom's Revised Taxonomy (Anderson) 11
Bloom's Taxonomy 12
Bonk, C. J. 39
Boysen, Guy A. 1, 39, 53
Brainscape 14

CANVA 19
case-based instruction 39
catalog description 10
CCOMFE model for online course design *15*, 15–16, 20

civic engagement 13
classroom: discussions 26; interactions 38
coaching/mentoring 39
cognitive map: of course content 14; for students 15
collaborative learning 5, 31–33, 39–41
college teachers 2
communication 13
communicative device 36
community-building method 24
concept map 19
content 30
cooperative online learning 31–33, 39
course: content 5, 7–8, 10–11, 14–16, 24, 27, 31; design 14–17, 50–51; modality 10
COVID-19 pandemic 10, 23
critical thinking 5, 13

debates 31
design 14–17
Digital Badges 42
Disciplinary Based Educational Research (DBER) 3
discipline-specific content 13
discipline-specific expertise 4
discussion boards 55
discussion forums 24
Dylan, Bob 26

engagement 15–16; active student 5, 42–43, 55; civic 13
evaluation 45–47, 50, 52, 57–59; and assessment 5; directness 5; formative evaluation 54; model online teachers (MoT) 46; utility 5

Index 67

evidence-informed instructional strategies 36
evidence-informed practices 1–3, 5, 36

face-to-face interactions 36; classes 16, 25; classroom assessment 20; learning 5; teachers 4; *see also* in-person interactions
Floyd, George 13, 34
formative evaluation 54

Glazier, R. A. 44
Gonzalez-Flores, P. 24
Google Forms 46
Google Voice 42
grades: assignments in online courses 52; and rubric scores 29
guided learning 39

Homa, N. 14–15
homework forums 31

Idorecall 14
Illinois Online Network Quality Online Course Initiative 59
improvement-focused assessment process 57
inclusive classroom 34
infographics 19
in-person interactions: classes 7; discussions 55; instructors 6; teaching 23; *see also* face-to-face interactions
instructional design(ers) 3, 15
instructional methods 3, 5, 20–21, 39–41
instructional shift 10
instructor behavioral learning objectives 36
instructor-to-student interaction 8, 36; instructional methods and skills 39–41; MoT checklist for 47–48; online teaching skills, practice effective 41–44; student evaluations of teaching 45–46; student feedback 46–47; syllabus, use of 36–39; synchronous/asynchronous learning 44–45
in-the-moment flexibility 6

jigsaw activities 31
Johnson, G. M. 45
just-in-time-teaching 5, 40–41

Kahoot! 40, 43
Keeley, J. 41

Keys, J. 38
Kim, K. J. 39

learner-centered approach 5, 14
learner-centered communication 37
learning-focused planning 50
learning management system (LMS) 11, 13–14, 43, 51; automatization 55; course content 13
learning objective communication 50–51
learning objectives: alignment 51–53; communicating 50–51; writing 52
learning sciences 3
lecture-based teacher-directed instruction 39
liberal arts skills 5
Loom 42

Martin, F. 40
mastery 4
McCabe, M. F. 24
Meyers, S. A. 44
microlearning apps 42
mind maps 19
modalities 6
model online teachers (MoTs) 1–2, 6–8, 15, 39, 43; CCOMFE model for online course design *15*, 15–16; checklist for instructor-to-student interaction 47–48; clarity 15; compassion 15; constructive feedback to students 28–29; course assignments 52; course material 26–27; design classes 16; design courses 49; engagement 15; evaluations 46; feedback to students 54; flexibility 15; multiple facets 15; organization 15; student discussion 26; student-to-student interaction 24
model teachers 4; course content 5; pedagogical expertise 4; syllabus 5; synchronous and asynchronous interactions 36; *see also* model online teachers (MoTs)
model teaching criteria 1–3, 7, 39; assessment 3, *4*; checklist for training 8; course content 3, *4*; defined 3–5; framework 1–2; instructional methods 3, *4*, 5; online teacher 1–2, 7–8; student evaluations 3, *4*; and sub-criteria *4*; syllabus design 3, *4*; tips for learning 9; training 3, *4*
module format, style and structure 18
multi-media learning 40–41
multiple-choice exam 13

68 *Index*

National Institution for Learning
  Outcomes Assessment (NILOA) 59
Novak, G. M. 40

online assessment 49; assessing student
  learning online 50–52; communicating
  learning objectives 50–51; constructive
  feedback online 53–55; learning
  objectives, assignments, and activities
  51–53; making assessment-based
  changes 56; Model Online Teaching
  Checklist 59; online instruction 49–59;
  teaching effectiveness assessment
  process 56–59
online campuses 3
online classes/courses 1, 6–7, 10, 13–14,
  17, 19, 24, 54; graded assignments in
  52–53; syllabus 36
online collaboration 25
online discussion 27; analysis prompt
  28; application prompt 28; effective
  26; facilitation 25–26; fostering
  collaboration 26; ineffective prompt
  28; synthesis prompt 28; writing
  instructions 28
online field trips 31
online instruction 31
online interactions with content 19–20
online rapport 44
online survey tool 46
online teachers 4
online teaching: approximating 10;
  course design choices 31; efficacy 1;
  instructional methods 5; merit 1
online tutoring 38

Pavlov's theory of classical
  conditioning 28
pedagogical training 2
peer-evaluation 9
practice effective online teaching skills
  41–44
Preparing Future Faculty 4
problem-based learning 5, 39
professional ethics 53
professionalism 30

Quality Matters 16; certification 59;
  training 17
quantitative literacy 13
Quizlet 14, 40, 42

rapport 1, 23, 43–46; *see also* online
  rapport

responsiveness to others 30
Riggs, Shannon 19
role-playing 39
rubrics 29–31
Ryan, R. G. 43

scholarship of teaching and learning
  (SoTL) 3
screen recording apps 42
self-evaluation 9
self-testing apps 42
shared case studies 31
Skinner's theory of operant
  conditioning 28
social bookmarking 31
socialization 24
social media 26
Society for the Teaching of Psychology 2
Socratic discussion 39
Stein, D. S. 25
Stommel, J. 25
straight-discussion teachers 39
student conduct code 34
student evaluations 23, 58
student feedback 46, 50
student-instructor contact 26
student interaction with content 10;
  continued learning, tips for 22; course
  design, structure, and clarity 14–17;
  instructional methods 20–21; model
  online teachers and course templates
  17–19; model online teaching
  checklist 21; online interactions
  with content 19–20; student learning
  objectives 10–13; syllabus and your
  LMS 13–14
student learning 5; with online discussion
  26–31; outcomes 15
student learning objectives (SLOs) 11,
  39–40; APA and 11–12; backwards
  design 12; based for psychology 12;
  for majors and minors 11
student learning outcomes 15
student-led teaching awards 23
student-teacher rapport 5
student-to-content interaction 8
student-to-student interaction 19;
  collaborative and cooperative
  online learning opportunities
  31–33; community of learners
  necessitates mitigation 33–34; conflict
  33–34; discussion expectations,
  communication 25–26; discussion
  forums 23–31; model online teaching

checklist 35; student community with online discussion 24–25; student learning with online discussion 26–31
Sulik, G. 38
Sull, E. C. 44
summative evaluations 52–53
SUNY Online Course Quality Review 59
Survey Monkey 46
syllabi 5, 15, 38, 39
syllabus *4*, 13–14, 21, 36–39, 47
symphonies 24
synchronous learning 44–45
synchronous polling apps 42

taxonomy 11–12
Taylor, Breonna 13
teacher-centered communication 37
teachers: face-to-face interactions 4; model teachers 4–5, 36; online 4; online course design 24; straight-discussion teachers 39; *see also* model online teachers (MoTs)
teaching effectiveness assessment process 56–59

teaching philosophy 37
team-based problem solving 31
team-based research projects 32
technological competence 5
TEDx Talks 40
Tempelman-Kluit, N. 40
texting apps 42
timeliness 30
training 4–5, 7, 8; pedagogical 2; Quality Matters 17
Tuning Project 11

Universal Design for Learning (UDL) 20–21

video conferencing apps 42
VoiceThread 31

Wanstreet, C. E. 25
wikis 31
Wilson, J. H. 43

YouTube 40

Zoom 42